Experiencing Music Composition
in Grades 3–5

Experiencing Music Composition

Michele Kaschub and Janice Smith
Series Editors

Experiencing Music Composition in Grades 3–5
Michele Kaschub & Janice Smith

Experiencing Music Composition in Grades 3–5

Michele Kaschub & Janice Smith

OXFORD
UNIVERSITY PRESS

OXFORD
UNIVERSITY PRESS

Oxford University Press is a department of the University of Oxford. It furthers
the University's objective of excellence in research, scholarship, and education
by publishing worldwide. Oxford is a registered trade mark of Oxford University
Press in the UK and certain other countries.

Published in the United States of America by Oxford University Press
198 Madison Avenue, New York, NY 10016, United States of America.

Library of Congress Cataloging-in-Publication Data
Names: Kaschub, Michele, 1967– | Smith, Janice, 1952–
Title: Experiencing music composition in grades 3–5 / Michele Kaschub and
Janice Smith.
Description: New York, NY : Oxford University Press, [2017] | Includes
bibliographical references and index.
Identifiers: LCCN 2016005842 | ISBN 9780190497644 (hbk. : alk. paper) |
ISBN 9780190497651 (pbk. : alk. paper)
Subjects: LCSH: Composition (Music)—Instruction and study |
Music—Instruction and study.
Classification: LCC MT40 .K277 2016 | DDC 372.87/4—dc23
LC record available at http://lccn.loc.gov/2016005842

9 8 7 6 5 4 3 2 1

Paperback printed by Webcom, Inc., Canada
Hardback printed by Bridgeport National Bindery, Inc., United States of America

CONTENTS

ABOUT THE COMPANION WEBSITE

www.oup.com/us/experiencingmusiccompositioningrades3to5
Username: Music3
Password: Book3234

Oxford has created a password-protected website to accompany *Experiencing Music Composition in Grades 3–5*. Full-color versions of each *Sketchpage* are provided so that teachers may project these images when facilitating classroom instruction or guiding whole-class composition activities. Black and white versions of each *Sketchpage* are provided so that teachers may print and distribute them to students.

PART I
Introduction to
Experiencing Music Composition

WELCOME TO
EXPERIENCING MUSIC COMPOSITION!

Composing music is a wonderful experience for children. It allows them to discover their musical imaginations as they create songs and pieces to suit their needs and interests and which they can share with others. Often people think that children need extensive formal training in music theory or considerable skill as performers to compose, but we have found that just about everyone can create music with a little help and some useful strategies. This book offers exactly that. It provides guidance for teachers who are ready to nurture creative spirits and suggests tools young composers can use to capture and manage their many musical ideas.

You do not have to be a professional composer to guide children as they create their own music, but some formal music training can be helpful. Active listening skills, a willingness to explore and consider a broad range of musical possibilities, some practice at asking critical questions of young composers about their work, and a strong belief that music will emerge from what may appear to be a busy, messy, and sometimes rather loud sound environment are all you need. These skills and dispositions combined with a focused approach will allow you and your students to find musical satisfaction and ongoing success.

In the following sections we will introduce the *Experiencing Music Composition* approach and present a snapshot of young composers and their work across Grades 3–5. The teaching and learning tools of *Experiencing Music Composition* can be used by composers of all ages to develop capacities critical in creating original music. These three capacities—*feelingful intention, musical expressivity*, and *artistic craftsmanship*—provide the springboard that advances children's work from collections of random sounds and brief musical gestures to thoughtfully created, expressive pieces. The *Sketchpages* are graphic organizers that guide students in thinking through their compositional ideas. They are included with every lesson to support the development of musical artistry. Each lesson also includes suggestions for productive sharing and feedback in a variety of formats to help composers assess their progress and evaluate the quality of their work.

We are excited that you and your young musicians are embarking on an exciting journey in creating original music and we hope that you will love *Experiencing Music Composition!*

Sincerely,

Michele Kaschub

Michele Kaschub

and

Janice P. Smith

Janice P. Smith

THE *EXPERIENCING MUSIC COMPOSITION* PROGRAM

Experiencing Music Composition is focused on providing opportunities for K–12 students to create original music through composition. The approach progresses from teacher-facilitated collaborative work, through partnered and small group activities, toward projects for which the students assume complete artistic autonomy. The lessons and activities of the program are designed to challenge students' skills and understandings as they explore the expressive potentials of sound across different genres, settings, and media.

The *Experiencing Music Composition* program is suitable for use in private teaching studios, school music programs, and any other place where young people make music. The compositional tasks of the program parallel those undertaken by singer-songwriters, movie score composers, video game score composers, commercial jingle creators, and everything in between. Students create songs, works for chorus and instrumental ensembles, pieces partnered with electronic media, music to accompany art installations, film, music theater, and much, much more.

Graphic organizers, called *Sketchpages,* guide and enhance this work. They are designed specifically to promote student creativity and develop key compositional skills. *Sketchpages* are a mix of doodle space and composer's notebook. As students work with these pages, they are invited to imagine how their music might sound and how others may experience those sounds as performers and listeners. Students quickly learn to identify and develop the feelings, thoughts, and ideas they wish to explore and share through their work. Further, they learn to use the tools and techniques of composition expressively to achieve artistic ends.

The *Experiencing Music Composition* approach promotes individuality. Students are encouraged to create music in a manner that reveals their unique musical ideas. This signature sound is often referred to as the composer's "voice." Just as many musical listeners easily recognize works of Aaron Copland, Ludwig van Beethoven, James Taylor or Taylor Swift, so will members of your musical community be able to identify pieces that "belong" to a specific composer or group of collaborative composers. The emergence of "voice" is important because it reveals a clarity of music thought and the capacity to engage meaningfully with music over time.

While individual voice is an important development for any artist, isolation rarely leads to meaningful growth. The *Experiencing Music Composition* program emphasizes collaborative learning, facilitated sharing, and productive feedback through Composer's Circles—a forum in which composers may share their work and ask other members of the community for reactions, advice, and suggestions. As composers interact with peers, teachers, performers, and others from the musical community at large, they are exposed to a broad palette of compositional tools, techniques, and ideas that may shape or influence not only their current project but future projects as well. This social format provides an important counterpart to work that may be isolating and helps composers balance subjective and objective evaluations of their own work.

And finally, the lessons and activities of the *Experiencing Music Composition* program can work seamlessly with the 2014 Core Music Standards[1] addressing Creativity in K–8 and Music Theory/Composition in grades 9–12. Each lesson touches on the Enduring Understandings and Essential Questions outlined within the standards while leaving open the specific compositional path. This kind of music learning is personally relevant and driven by each student's curiosities and passions within music. The compositional challenges that students face are authentic and true to the experience of composition in the world at large.

Note

1 2014 Core Music Standards created by the National Association for Music Education in the United States are available at http://www.nafme.org/my-classroom/standards/core-music-standards/.

WHAT TO EXPECT FROM YOUNG COMPOSERS

The music that young composers create springs from their lived experiences and their imaginations. They are drawn to both the familiar and the novel and they enjoy borrowing musical material and folding it into their work. In many ways these attributes make them like all composers throughout history, but composers in Grades 3–5 also have attributes specific to their level of development. The following descriptions of young composers and their music may help you determine what is appropriate and useful in guiding the work of young composers.

Typical Characteristics of Composers in Grades 3–5

♪ Young composers may be engaged in music making as performers by singing in choirs, or beginning instrumental study. These experiences are likely to influence compositional processes and products.

♪ Young composers hear music in their imaginations and need help figuring out how to transfer sounds from their imaginations to the outside world.

♪ Young composers explore compositional techniques by imitating ideas found in peer work or other musical models.

♪ Young composers need to be encouraged to try new things and trust their own judgments.

♪ Young composers have definite musical preferences.

♪ Young composers tend to organize musical ideas horizontally, but vertical organizations and more complex textures and harmonies begin to occur purposefully as overall compositional experience grows.

♪ Young composers think about how they react to music.

♪ Young composers are beginning to think about how listeners may react to particular sounds and organizations of sounds.

♪ Young composers have a sense of musical humor and enjoy the element of surprise.

♪ Young composers want their audience to "get it."

Typical Qualities of Works by Composers in Grades 3–5

♪ Compositions often feature quotes of familiar pieces that are well known to, and liked by, the composer.

♪ Compositions may prominently feature repetition as it both provides unity and is a useful tool to boost memory prior to the creation of written scores.

♪ Compositions tend to be quite brief—which also makes them easy to remember.

♪ Compositions are often lively and full of motion.

♪ Compositions make use of tension to achieve surprise or other types of big impact.

♪ Compositions are often performance driven, with musical choices and sound organizations tightly intertwined with the notion of "who-plays-what-when" in group settings.

♪ Compositions favor predictability.

♪ Compositions connect to daily life in concrete ways.

HOW TO USE THIS BOOK

Section 1 Compositional Capacities	Section 2 Using *Sketchpages*
Section 3 Creating Positive Compositional Experiences	Section 4 Teacher Guides & Student *Sketchpages*

This book is divided into four sections. Each section offers insights and tools for working with young composers. Section 1 introduces the key focus of the *Experiencing Music Composition* approach—the three compositional capacities that are the foundation of the composer's work. Numerous examples and resources are provided to prepare teachers to guide students in developing specific skills and abilities related to each compositional capacity.

Section 2 focuses on the use of *Sketchpages*. These graphic organizers serve as creative spaces for students to use when planning compositions, actively composing, or reflecting on their work. *Sketchpages* can be used to organize group work or to help individual composers as they consider the music they wish to create. *Sketchpages* can also be useful data collection tools because they reveal the connections that students make between the three compositional capacities.

The music that young composers create represents a deeply personal investment. Sharing music with others places young composers in a vulnerable position. Section 3 offers guidance and strategies for sharing work, providing feedback, and encouraging future growth in a manner that fosters a positive learning environment and honors each composer's musical autonomy.

Section 4 contains teacher guides with ready-to-use *Sketchpages* to get you and your young composers creating original music in five different compositional genres. Each guide outlines one or more possible approaches to the lesson. They are intended to help you get started and to serve as models.

PART II
Facilitating the Work of Young Composers

1

Compositional Capacities

On Composing

All students have the ability to create music that is uniquely their own. The act of composing transcends the limits of verbal and mathematical representations and allows children to explore sound as a means for sharing who they are, what they think, and what they feel about their experiences in the world. It invites them to draw on the full breadth of their musical skills and understanding to create music that represents their unique insights. As such, composition is more than just an activity of music education; it is a process that draws together intellect and intuition, thinking and feeling, and the practical and the inspired. It brings into reality thoughts and feelings that have only existed in the imagination and contributes to the creation of our individual and collective human spirit.

Just as some students find spelling easier than others—or read with greater comprehension or solve math problems more quickly—some children will have a more developed sense of music composition. Students' abilities depend on natural aptitude and the opportunities and the instruction they have had. Throughout *Experiencing Music Composition,* activities will focus on the development of three compositional capacities: feelingful intention, musical expressivity, and artistic craftsmanship. Each plays an integral role in the way we experience and understand music.

Feelingful Intention

Many times children create musical motifs or short, repetitive pieces completely by chance. Teachers who recognize these fledgling compositions can encourage young composers to create more of them. As children develop music beyond these initial ideas, they can be guided to think about how their music makes them feel and how it might make others feel. The ability to consider the emotional impact of musical sounds is the capacity of *feelingful intention.*

Children know that music has the ability to communicate because they have encountered music that has aroused feelings in them. Simply suggesting to a child that she create some music that conveys the impression of a familiar feeling can lead to a composition that is more expressive than one rooted in writing music notation.

For example, a group of third graders come to music class very excited about the baby chicks that are hatching in their classroom's incubator. The teacher listens to their stories and recognizes their excitement as an opportunity to compose. She suggests that the students create music about the way they feel as they watch the chicks emerge. Some of the students suggest a different perspective, that of the chicks breaking free of their eggshells.

Instruments are selected and the sounds of musical thinking soon fill the room. The teacher hears rhythmic ostinatos, rising and falling melodies, and a few simple harmonies emerging from various spots around the room. When the students share their pieces, the teacher asks questions that help them identify how they have crafted their music. The names for these techniques can then be introduced and added to an ongoing list of compositional strategies that any composer may use to invite particular feelingful responses.

Developing the Capacity of Feelingful Intention

The intention to create music that sounds like feelings feel is implicit in all music. It is the *why* of music composition and the gateway to using compositional tools and techniques with artistic purpose. Young musicians are aware of the feelingful impact of the music that they encounter, but their awareness may be more tacit than explicit. Below are some activities that may be used to help students develop the capacity of feelingful intention.

- ♪ Ask students to describe the feeling they have when they listen to a particular piece of music. Follow up with "What about the music makes you feel that way?" Remind the students that well-crafted music can invite different responses, so there may be many different answers.

- ♪ Build a chart of words with the students that can be used to describe moods, feelings and impressions. A sample is shown in Figure 1.1. Students will have greater ownership in a resource that they contribute to creating and will use it more frequently than a teacher's handout or pre-made poster.

- ♪ Encourage students to experiment with different feelingful intentions when they perform. If a single phrase is played with opposite intentions, does the music and their feeling about it change? In what way?

- ♪ Invite students to spend 10–15 minutes listening to and analyzing one of their own playlists. Do they notice a common feelingful intention? A string of related intentions? A highly varied list? What do they think about what they have observed? Does a similar list of feelingful intention descriptors fit the music they have composed? Why or why not?

- ♪ Play "feelingful intention grab bag." Write feelingful intention descriptors on small pieces of paper and have students draw them out of a hat. Have students spend 2 minutes composing a short melodic idea that they believe captures the feeling of the descriptive word. Have the students perform their ideas (for the whole group or for a partner) and explain what they did in trying to invite a particular feelingful response.

- ♪ Composers often write verbal introductions to pieces or may have left letters or other written documents describing their work. Share some of these with students after listening to a piece. In what ways did the students' experiences of the piece match or differ from what the composer had envisioned?

- ♪ Encourage students to identify the feelingful intention or intentions in their own work as well as in the work of their peers. Feelingful intentions may be outlined in planning stages of the compositional process or may emerge organically as students explore and test their many musical ideas as a piece unfolds. Building an awareness of feelingful intention and its role in shaping musical decision making is a key component in the artistic development of young composers.

Figure 1.1

Words for describing feelingful intentions

adorable	dramatic	hot	nasty	scary	tough
adventurous	dreary	huge	naughty	scratchy	tragic
afraid	dull	humble	needy	serene	tricky
amazing	eager	hungry	negative	serious	trusting
amused	electric	icky	nervous	sharp	ugly
angry	elegant	imaginative	nice	shimmering	understated
anxious	embarrassed	impish	numb	shiny	unique
awesome	enchanted	important	nutty	shrill	united
awful	energetic	impossible	odd	shy	unlucky
awkward	envious	innocent	orderly	sick	unpleasant
beautiful	evil	intelligent	ornate	silent	unruly
bold	exciting	irritating	outlandish	silly	unsteady
boring	exotic	jagged	overjoyed	simple	upset
bossy	fabulous	jazzy	overlooked	sizzling	useful
bouncy	fancy	jealous	pale	sleepy	vast
brave	fantastic	jittery	passionate	slow	velvety
bright	fast	jolly	peaceful	small	vibrant
broken	fat	joyous	perky	smooth	vicious
bubbly	feisty	jumpy	pesky	sneaky	victorious
bumpy	flowery	kind	plain	soft	villainous
busy	fluffy	klutzy	playful	somber	violent
calm	fluid	kooky	pompous	soulful	vivacious
careful	forceful	lazy	posh	stiff	vivid
charming	formal	light	powerful	stormy	warlike
cheerful	fresh	little	precious	strange	warm
clever	friendly	lively	pretty	strident	wary
clumsy	frightened	lonely	prickly	strong	watery
cold	funny	lopsided	proud	sturdy	wavy
confident	fussy	loud	pushy	stylish	weak
comfortable	fuzzy	loving	puzzled	surprised	weary
confused	gentle	low	quaint	sweet	weepy
courageous	giant	loyal	quarrelsome	sympathetic	weighty
creepy	glamorous	lucky	quick	tame	weird
crisp	glittering	lumpy	quiet	tedious	wet
crowded	gloomy	mad	quirky	tempting	whimsical
cruel	gorgeous	magnificent	radiant	tender	wicked
cuddly	graceful	majestic	ragged	tense	wide
curly	grateful	marvelous	rapid	terrible	wiggly
curvy	gross	massive	reckless	terrific	wild
cute	gruesome	mean	regal	thankful	wise
dangerous	grumpy	meek	reliable	thick	witty
daring	happy	mellow	rich	thin	wobbly
dark	harsh	memorable	rigid	thorny	woeful
deep	haunting	menacing	robust	thoughtful	wonderful
defiant	heavy	merry	rough	thunderous	young
delicate	high	messy	rowdy	tidy	youthful
delightful	hollow	misty	royal	tight	yummy
dizzy	hopeful	murky	sad	tiny	zany
dope	horrible	mysterious	safe	tired	zesty

Musical Expressivity

Music's expressive power relies on our ability to perceive the continually shifting balances within and between motion and stasis, unity and variety, sound and silence, tension and release, and stability and instability. These five musical principles, which we term "M.U.S.T.S.," correspond directly to the way we perceive changes in our condition and environment through the complex array of our internal and external senses. When children understand this connection, they learn to reference their own intuitive understandings and can draw on a personal bank of feelings that have arisen in their own experiences to consider how sound might be shaped to invite similar feelings. This skill allows composers to strategically select and shape how feelings are *sonified*—expressed in sound.

Continuing with our peeping chick example, some young composers might recall half holding their breath in excitement as the faint pecking of the chicks becomes louder and louder until a shell finally breaks (increasing sound, decreasing relative silence). Some composers might try to organize sounds that parallel the feeling of anticipation (tension) that accompanied the chicks' transformation from wet to fluffy. Other composers might sonify the feeling of excitement brought about by the gentle cacophony of multiple chicks hatching and beginning to peep and move about all at once (from relative stasis to more movement). While each composer may pursue a different feelingful intention or focus on a different aspect of the experience, musical expressivity can be achieved if students are encouraged to use sounds in a balance that "feels right."

More about the M.U.S.T.S.

The five principle pairs that comprise the M.U.S.T.S. can be found in our experience of a wide variety of music. While one or more of the principle pairs may be more prominent than others in a given work or section of a piece, all five are usually present in varying degree. Beyond presence or absence, it is the change in relational balance within each pair that gives rise to music's expressive potential. Let's consider how each principle pair functions.

Motion and Stasis: People move in lots of different ways. They can climb, walk, jump, run, amble, or meander. Eventually, they will pause or even completely stop. Music, too, may contain moments of considerable motion, moments of stasis, and moments that are of any degree in between. If we were to use a slider to represent the relational balance for a piece with an A-section of running sixteenth notes, it might look like Figure 1.2.

Figure 1.2

Relational balance favoring motion

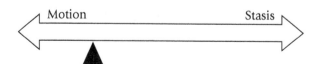

A slower moving B-section might be better represented as shown in Figure 1.3.

Figure 1.3

Relational balance
favoring stasis

17

Motion   Stasis

Most important, the A and B sections are perceived to have more motion or more stasis through comparison to each other. It is important to remember that comparisons are not limited to those made within a single piece but extend to all of the other musical pieces that a listener knows and can reference.

Unity and Variety: People look for patterns in nearly everything. The brain finds repetition to be highly satisfying but also seeks novelty to hold its attention in a different way. Most music uses a balance of unity and variety to create comfort as well as to pique and hold our interest. While unity and variety can be achieved through any of music's components, striking just the right balance can be tricky. Too much of the same thing may cause a listener to lose interest just as too many novel ideas may also overwhelm.

Sound and Silence: Sound is ubiquitous in daily life, yet the presence or absence of a particular sound can define the focus of our attention. In some cases, a single type of sound can become so familiar that it begins to function as an "attentional constant." Air circulation devices, humming lights, passing traffic, and other environmental sounds are examples of sounds we often ignore until we notice their absence. In this way, silence plays an important role as it can provide an opportunity to reframe and prioritize what we are hearing.

Consider these two graphic representations of sound (gray) and silence (white). In the upper half of Figure 1.4, a brass quintet delivers sound and silence in opposition so that the actions of the group are perceived as a whole. In the lower half of the figure, a shifting balance between sound and silence appears in the Trumpet 2 line against constant sound from the other members of the quintet. This structure may draw the listener to pay closer attention to the ideas delivered by the second trumpet while the supporting ideas offered by the remainder of the group assume more of a background position.

Figure 1.4

Relational balances between sound and silence

Trumpet 1																			
Trumpet 2																			
Fr. Horn																			
Trombone																			
Tuba																			

Trumpet 1																			
Trumpet 2																			
Fr. Horn																			
Trombone																			
Tuba																			

These are just two of many ways that sound and silence can be shaped to influence how we feel as we engage with music.

Tension and Release: Apprehension, excitement, and maybe a little nervousness often precede big life events. Such events are often followed with a certain sense of relief. Music, too, can offer parallel experiences as tension grows and releases through the way sounds are shaped. Like unity and variety, nearly any aspect of music can be shaped to invite tension or provide release. A gradually expanding instrumentation, a steadily building dynamic, or a halting rhythmic figure embedded within a repetitive rhythmic framework can all produce tension and each can be countered to provide release in equal measure.

Stability and Instability: Finally, when life unfolds as expected, we feel stable and safe. However, when there are surprises or challenges, we can begin to feel unsettled. Music, too, can have moments of stability or feel unsettled as it searches for firm ground. Music that extends too far into stability or instability is generally considered unpleasant. Stability quickly becomes tedious as there is nothing new to sustain attention and curiosity, while instability grows tiresome as the listener has to work too hard to stay engaged. Striking just the right balance between familiar and novel is a challenge pursued by composers in every genre.

Developing the Capacity of Musical Expressivity

Music teachers often focus on the elements of music (dynamics, form, harmony, melody, texture, tone color, and rhythm) as a means of making performances more expressive. Ironically, focusing exclusively on the elements in creating new music can lead to a lack of artistry. For example, asking a student to create a piece that contains a tempo change may allow the teacher to determine whether the student understands the concept of tempo, but the inclusion of a tempo change in and of itself does not guarantee that the music will evoke a feelingful response.

Framing the compositional task in a manner that connects experience and feeling is a more effective approach. For example, a student might be invited to create a piece of music that unfolds like a foot race. As the young composers think about what it is like to run a race and consider how racing is experienced in the body, they are likely to explore form and changing tempo in a way that both reveals their conceptual understandings and leads to the creation of a work that features motion–stasis, tension–release, and perhaps other principles, too. In this way, the elements are not artificially strung together but emerge as a natural part of the bigger picture that allows for expressive music to be made.

It is important to help students discover overarching and site specific feelingful intentions and musical expressivities. The M.U.S.T.S. can be applied at the level of the whole composition, to just a section of the work, or even across a single phrase or measure. In creating the "racing music" described above, a composer might aim to create a composition that builds from a very stable, almost static beginning to a tension-filled climatic conclusion. Within that framework, there might be a section of the piece built on repetition at ever-increasing volume levels and higher speeds. The melody for that section might feature a series of rising pitched motives that help create the feeling of tension. Thus tension, and most likely its subsequent release, occurs at the level of the whole composition, the section, and the phrase. Multi-level application may not suit all compositions, but students can be encouraged to think about the M.U.S.T.S. to maximize the expressive potential of their music as is appropriate to their particular goals.

Artistic Craftsmanship

Artistic craftsmanship is the capacity to purposefully shape and organize sounds in a musically expressive manner that invites feelingful response. Composers need to familiarize themselves with a wide range of tools and master a considerable body of techniques to develop fluency in artistic craftsmanship, but this takes time and careful guidance. When techniques are taught before feelingful intentions and musical expressivities have been considered, the compositional process becomes a mere technical exercise.

Young composers provided with a lesson on range can create a piece of music that explores high and low pitches, but they may not be moved to use those pitches in an artistic manner. Conversely, if the young composers working on the chick-inspired pieces use a bass xylophone to recall pecking, a small xylophone to parallel peeping, and play several pitches simultaneously in close proximity to suggest the idea of multiple chicks peeping at once, the teacher can introduce range and tone clusters as compositional tools. Teaching composition with a focus on capacities provides opportunities for discovery. Students can be led to see connections between specific techniques and their feelingful and expressive impact. This promotes artistry and artistic thinking.

The phrase "tools and techniques of artistic craftsmanship" will appear throughout *Experiencing Music Composition.* "Tools" are those internal and external devices that influence and shape how young composers think. Internal tools include the musical imagination and inner hearing. Activities that encourage students to imagine sound and to manipulate those sounds foster the skills that allow composers to work without external sound sources. Similarly, systems that enable the imagination of sound through the use of symbols for pitch (solfeggio) or time (counting systems) also facilitate the composers' abilities to organize and shape sound in their minds.

External compositional tools include anything external to the composer that helps facilitate thinking. This may include instruments; computers; voices; smart devices; software, applications, or web-based programs; lined and unlined manuscript paper; iconic, invented, or standardized notational systems; and recording devices. Tool choices change and evolve over time to suit the needs of the composer and the music being created. It is important that students experience a wide range of internal and external tools as they develop their personal vocabularies of composition.

"Technique" is the manner in which composers shape sound. It includes choices and decisions about how to use pitch, time, space, dynamics, form, instrumentation, and orchestration, texture, and articulation. Technique is best developed through exposure, recognition, and purposeful introduction as well as through singing, playing, listening or improvising, recognition and purposeful introduction, and compositional experimentation.

Techniques and Etudes for Grades 3–5

While it is beyond the scope of this volume to address all the possible techniques that young composers may encounter or utilize in their work, the following material will foster the development of artistic craftsmanship. The etudes suggested below range from initial explorations for first-time composers to more advanced challenges suitable for experienced fifth grade students. Etudes serve to teach students about possible techniques that they may use in future composing projects. Young composers often benefit from instruction that introduces etudes once they have expressed an interest in a particular technique or perceived a "need to know" moment in their own work.

The following labels are used to indicate the level of difficulty for each etude:

(B) Beginner level etudes are appropriate for students with little to no previous composing experience.

(I) Intermediate level etudes are appropriate for students with some previous experience.

(A) Advanced level etudes contain challenging techniques for experienced composers.

Pitch

Young composers should be encouraged to experiment and play with different modes, melodic constructs, and harmonies as a way to understand the impact of pitch on how music is experienced.

Modes

♪ Create compositions using major, minor, pentatonic (B), chromatic, whole tone (I), invented (B), and other scales (A)

♪ Use a single mode throughout a piece (B); use two modes in a single piece (I)

Melodies

♪ Invent a motive (B) and repeat or vary it throughout a piece (I)

♪ Explore five different melodic shapes: pitches moving up, pitches moving down, smile (high to low to high), frown (low to high to low), and same (intervals remain static) (B)

♪ Experiment with different types of motion—steps, skips, or leaps (B)

♪ Create a piece that is limited to a single type of motion, uses just two, or includes all three (I)

♪ Reconstruct a stepwise melody to create a melody with larger intervals through intervallic expansion (I)

♪ Decorate a melody with additional notes—ornamentation (B)
♪ Remove notes from a melody—truncation (B)
♪ Alter a melody by substituting different pitches or replacing pitches with rests (B)
♪ Rewrite an existing melody backward—retrograde (I)
♪ Flip an existing melody upside down—inversion (A)
♪ Create a new melody over an existing chord progression (I)

Harmony

♪ Invent a repeating harmonic pattern to underpin or accompany a melody (B)
♪ Create a descant to fit an existing melody (A)
♪ Add a countermelody to a previously composed melody (A)
♪ Create a partner song for an existing song (A)
♪ Explore harmonic boundaries by limiting works to single chords or using only tonic and dominant (I)
♪ Explore chord progressions commonly found in specific genres, i.e., Blues, four-chord pop songs (A)

Time

Time is an organizing component of the musical experience used to measure the rate and duration of sounds. Musical time is revealed in the way beats are grouped metrically and subdivided to create rhythm. Composers also shape how we experience time through the use of tempo. Below are some ideas for exploring beat, meter, rhythm, and tempo.

Beat

♪ Explore music with and without a steady beat (B)
♪ Create music with strong and weak beats in predictable and unpredictable patterns (I)

Meter

♪ Create music in simple and/or compound meters (B)
♪ Convert a piece in simple meter to compound meter and vice versa (I)
♪ Experiment with the subdivision of the meter (B)
♪ Use multiple meters in a single work (I)

Rhythm

♪ Create simple and complex rhythms (B)
♪ Invent rhythmic ostinatos as accompaniment figures (B)
♪ Explore rhythmic variation by adding notes within the beat (I)
♪ Create syncopated rhythms (B)
♪ Alter rhythms by replacing pitches with rests (B)

♪ Layer rhythms to create percussion pieces (B)

♪ Explore duration through augmentation or diminution of rhythmic note values (I)

♪ Manipulate duration by reordering existing rhythms in retrograde (B)

Tempo

♪ Explore how tempo changes can impact the mood or feelingful character of a work (B)

♪ Incorporate multiple tempos within a single work (B)

♪ Explore nuanced changes in tempo through use of accelerando, rallentando, and rubato (I)

Space

Composers do not always control the spaces in which their compositions will be heard. However, composers may specify the ways in which performers are intended to position pieces and the ways that audiences should encounter them. Composers may give special thought to the locations in which their works will be performed, how performers will be physically placed within concert spaces, the mindset that performers and audiences might adopt when engaging with a work, and even storylines that imply other times and places. Some of these considerations are listed below.

Auditory Parameters

♪ Create instructions that direct performers to multiple locations within a performance space to alter audience perceptions, i.e., orchestra on stage, small groups of instrumentalists off stage, or situated behind the audience (I)

♪ Explore panning (left to right), frequencies (high to low), and intensity (close physical proximity to distant horizon) when positioning sounds to be played through speakers (I)

Conceptual Spaces

♪ Specify a performance space to capitalize on connotations that people bring to the space, i.e., the rowdiness of a school gymnasium versus the reverence at a war memorial (I)

♪ Write program notes that invoke a particular time, space, or set of conditions to frame a musical work or the audiences' experience of the work (B)

Performance Environment

♪ Specify the setup for a concert environment: performers on stage and listeners in the audience (B)

♪ Create instructions that require a participatory environment in which performers and listeners intermingle so that the audience is part of the performance (B)

♪ Make a work for a virtual environment. Performers and audience will connect virtually in real time or asynchronously (I)

♪ Create a work to be experienced through earbuds in an individual environment where specifications relate to panning (I)

Temporal Space

♪ Create an "extra-temporal" timeline through the use of program notes or lyrics that describe another time/space and seek to transport the audience into that world (I)

Dynamics

Dynamic levels within a work mark important changes in intensity and do not refer to decibel levels (volume). Changes in dynamics may be achieved in several different ways and influence how music is shaped by performers and experienced by listeners. Composers can manipulate dynamics by altering intensity, relationship, and balance.

Intensity

♪ Create varying degrees of intensity by changing written/performed dynamic levels (B)

♪ Explore changes in instrumentation: the more instruments, voices, or other sound sources contribute to a soundscape, the greater will be the intensity of the music (B)

♪ Use different combinations of instruments, voices, or other sound sources to capitalize on natural acoustic properties, i.e., children's voices produce sound waves that travel differently from the sound waves generated by a quartet of tubas (I)

Relational

♪ Offer sudden changes in character of the music through use of *subito* dynamics, i.e., *sfz—subito forzando*, "suddenly with force" (B)

♪ Create gradual changes in the character of the music through use of *crescendo* and *decrescendo* (B)

Balance and Blend

♪ Specify different dynamic levels for each instrument to increase or decrease presence within texture (I)

Form

Musical form refers to the overall architecture of musical sounds. Organization levels can be viewed from large structures (i.e., symphonies), to mid-level components (i.e., the "A" section), or smaller structures (i.e., phrases). The formal constructs below are listed from smallest to largest in scope.

Motive

♪ Create a melodic motive of at least four pitches and then explore the ways it may be varied by altering only the rhythm (B)

♪ Explore how the impact of a rhythm is altered when pitches are added—within a single pitch class, close intervals, distant intervals, etc. (I)

Phrase

♪ Extend a motive into a phrase through the use of sequence, motivic variation, or other elongation techniques (I)

♪ Transform a motive into an imitative gesture by passing it between two instruments or voices (B)

♪ Alter melodic contours and supporting harmonies to lengthen or shorten phrases (A)

♪ Experiment with varying the ending of the phrase to create different feelings—question, answer, uncertainty, surprise, etc. (I)

Period

♪ Explore half cadences and cadential elisions as ways of joining phrases to build periods (I)

Section

♪ Construct different formal structures such AB, ABA, AAB, ABB, Rondo, Blues, 32-bar song, and other forms (I)

Movement

♪ Create several shorter works with some unifying aspect that allows them to be grouped together into a longer work (A)

Full Work

♪ Consider the classification of the work identifying the specific genre, particular style, or performance practice (A)

♪ Draw connections between multiple works (A)

Instrumentation and Orchestration

Instrumentation is the choice of particular sounds or combination of sounds while orchestration refers to the way the instruments are used to create particular moods. Once a composer has selected instruments, orchestration may be more specifically tailored to invite particular affective response.

Sound Sources

♪ Select instruments, voices, or other sound sources to be used in music composition and explain why each was chosen for inclusion (B)

♪ Invent pieces for solo instrument, voice, or other sound source to focus on its particular abilities and idiomatic tendencies (A)

Timbre

♪ Explore the different qualities of an individual instrument, voice, or other sound source in terms of character and quality (I)

♪ Combine two or more instruments, voices, or other sound sources to explore the interrelationships between different characters and qualities of sound (B)

♪ Create pieces that use instruments from a single family—woodwind, brass, string, percussion, keyboard, electronic, etc. (I)

♪ Make a work that juxtaposes instruments from two or more different families (I)

Range

♪ Experiment with the full range of pitches (highest to lowest) available for a single or combination of instruments, voices, or other sound sources to determine the impact of outer margins versus center (A)

Register

♪ Create music that capitalizes on the tone quality of a particular instrument, voice, or other sound source

♪ Explore how different instruments, voices, or sound sources take on different qualities in different registers and how this influences combinations of instruments, voices, or other sound sources (A)

Tessitura

♪ Create music within a range of pitches that are appropriate—easy to produce and pleasant sounding—to specific instruments, voices, or other sound sources (I)

♪ Purposefully create music with pitches that are within the capacity, but beyond the "comfort zone," of specific instruments, voices, or other sound sources (A)

Texture

Texture refers to layers of sound. Texture may include how many independent and dependent musical lines are present, how many instruments or voices are in use, how many sounds are unfolding simultaneously, and the relative presence or absence of particular sounds in the piece at any given moment. Below are a few activities that explore different types of texture.

Monophonic

- ♪ Create unaccompanied melodies for solo and unison parts (B)
- ♪ Compose pieces that contrast unison sections with other textures (I)

Biphonic

- ♪ Create works with two distinct parts: one line is melodic, the other is simpler and serves as accompaniment (B)

Homophonic Movement

- ♪ Create works with two or more parts moving in identical rhythm, but with different pitches to imply chordal harmony (A)
- ♪ Use an existing harmonic progression to create a new work (I)
- ♪ Create works for solo instruments with simple chordal accompaniment (I)

Polyphonic Movement

- ♪ Create rounds and canons (I)
- ♪ Write countermelodies and descants to fit existing songs or original melodies (I)
- ♪ Explore counterpoint by creating intertwining melodies with and without accompaniment (A)

Articulation

Articulation refers to the way that musical sounds start and end. The use of specific attack and release types can contribute to the distinctive character of the musical style.

Attack

- ♪ Experiment with different ways of producing a sound, i.e., staccato, accent, tenuto, marcato, double or triple tonguing, flutter tongue, pizzicato, up bow, down bow, pluck, slap, hard versus soft mallets, etc. (B)

Release

- ♪ Explore different ways of ending sounds, i.e., arco, pizzicato, damped, fade out, etc. (B)

Developing the Capacity of Artistic Craftsmanship

Any of the preceding techniques of artistic craftsmanship can be taught as the need arises within the context of a composer's own work or as part of a class focusing on a specific tool or technique. In class settings, short lessons on new concepts or tools are often an effective way of moving a group of young composers forward to new possibilities. Such introductions should always be sound based. The students' own performance or recordings can be used to illustrate new compositional ideas and to bring into consideration how such ideas can be used to achieve expressive ends. Students can also be shown how such ideas might be notated in invented, iconographic, or traditional notation. By developing ear and eye together, students expand their compositional palette.

Final Thoughts

The capacities of feelingful intention, musical expressivity, and artistic craftsmanship may be discussed at nearly any point in the compositional process. The key point is that each must be brought into the conscious thought of young musicians for them to develop their ideas and to grow as composers. The capacities help students move beyond the "fortuitous accident" stage where they occasionally and unintentionally generate a satisfying musical idea to the point where they create by design. When students consider and deliberately use M.U.S.T.S. in their work, the tools and techniques they use serve as the sonic connection between lived experience and feeling. Those feelingful relationships often free young composers to think more expressively about music composition so that they may create artistic and personally meaningful work.

2

Using *Sketchpages*

Guiding the Journey

Have you ever taken a walk in an unfamiliar place and wondered if you would ever find your way? Composers often experience a similar degree of concern as they attempt to travel from musical idea to musical work. Within *Experiencing Music Composition,* compositional paths are illuminated through the use of *Sketchpages*—reproducible student guides that combine open doodle space, thinking prompts, and composer's notebooks.

Sketchpages accompany every lesson in this volume. They are designed to help students explore their musical ideas as they consider the connections between feelingful intention, musical expressivity, and artistic craftsmanship. The pages serve as inspirational spaces where students jot ideas during or between composing sessions. These ideas become points of reference and help students monitor their progress from initial imaginings through the final product. *Sketchpages* may be added to or revised by students as their compositional journey unfolds. Most important, the use of *Sketchpages* can remove the pressure to quickly arrive at an end product.

The main purpose of a *Sketchpage* is to provide a practical tool that composers can use to explore and develop the potential of their musical ideas. *Sketchpages* can be particularly helpful when teachers and students discuss musical ideas that exist primarily in the student's imagination. They offer a visual representation of key compositional ideas and relationships. This allows composers to pursue their own preferred working styles.

Each segment on the "A-side" of a *Sketchpage* corresponds to a compositional capacity. This allows teachers and students to begin with any capacity and connect outward toward the remaining two capacities. Whether composers are working with images or words, or using invented or traditional notation, *Sketchpages* can be used to capture compositional ideas ranging from motives to fully articulated, large-scale works. This helps composers manage the details of music creation in a productive manner.

The "B-side" of each *Sketchpage* can be tailored to match the notational skill level of young composers. In the appendices of this volume, there are four notation sheets that can be copied onto the back of *Sketchpages* or kept in piles where students may simply collect the sheet they need as they work. The invented notation page is primarily white space. The transitions sheets feature white space for invented notation and staff paper to use as students learn to notate their ideas. The final sheet is staff paper and suited to students who are comfortable with notating their ideas in the traditional manner.

Introducing *Sketchpages* to Young Composers

The best way to introduce the use of *Sketchpages* to young composers is to facilitate a teacher-guided whole-class composition activity (Lesson 3.1 begins this way). Whole group activities begin with the teacher projecting the *Sketchpage* so that all students can see it and work on it together. The teacher describes the composition task and invites students to discuss each of the guiding questions or prompts while noting student ideas and answers on the *Sketchpage*. With a little guidance, students should be able to work through a *Sketchpage* with a partner, in a small group, and eventually, by themselves.

When students first begin to use *Sketchpages*, they are likely to create simple one-to-one relationships in which they identify a single feelingful intention fulfilled through one of the principle pairs (M.U.S.T.S.) and crafted through the use of one or two techniques.

Figure 2.1 is a transcription of a piece created by a student contributing to a class musical collage entitled "Things That Happen in the Fall." The observation of a squirrel taking a cookie from a picnic table was the point of inspiration. The student described his feelingful intention as "mischievous," sought to express that through the use of motion and stasis, and crafted the music with eighth notes and half notes played with legato and staccato articulations. Figure 2.2 shows a graphic representation of these relationships.

Figure 2.1

Example of a teacher-transcribed student composition

Stealing a Cookie
Squirrel sneaking up to a picnic table

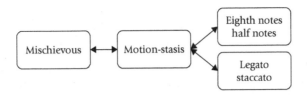

Figure 2.2

Graphic
representation of
capacities in simple
relationship

As student compositions become increasingly multi-faceted, graphic representations of their works reveal an ever-expanding array of connections. Figure 2.3 shows two diagrams of intermediate complexity while Figure 2.4 reveals the complex interconnections of a much more advanced work. Regardless of how simple or complex the connections between capacities may be, *Sketchpages* move learning forward.

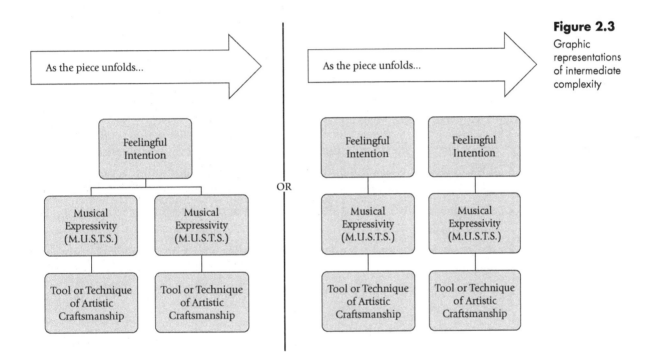

Figure 2.3

Graphic
representations
of intermediate
complexity

Figure 2.4

Complex graphic organizer

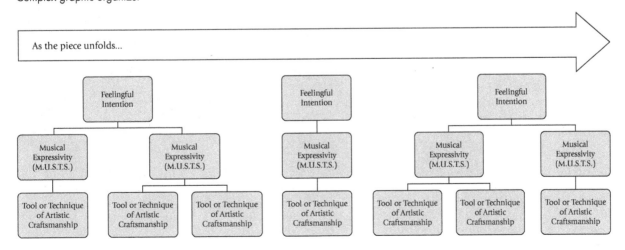

Sketchpages as Multi-taskers

Sketchpages can fill many roles as teachers and students work together in the classroom. Teachers can use *Sketchpages* to develop a better understanding of each student's needs as young composers use the graphic organizers to help them move musical ideas from their imaginations into the world.

Teachers can use *Sketchpages* to

- ♪ facilitate the development of each child's compositional capacities.
- ♪ encourage the development of critical and creative thinking skills as students imagine, execute, and reflect on their compositional ideas.
- ♪ gain a better understanding of each student's compositional processes.
- ♪ provide meaningful and specific feedback that respects the student's compositional goals.
- ♪ assess student work (in collaboration with the composer).

Students can use *Sketchpages* to

- ♪ remember key ideas and concepts essential to their feelingful intention.
- ♪ understand the relationship between feelingful intention musical expressivities/M.U.S.T.S., and the tools of artistic craftsmanship.
- ♪ apply their knowledge and skills to develop and extend initial ideas and conceptions.
- ♪ analyze problems and consider multiple solutions to a broad range of compositional challenges.
- ♪ evaluate a plan for solo, partnered, small group, or large group work.
- ♪ isolate specific compositional challenges.
- ♪ create expressive compositions that invite performers and audiences to meaningfully engage with music.

Creating Positive Compositional Experiences

The music that young composers create represents a deeply personal investment and may reveal an unguarded sharing of feelings and emotions. This creates a potentially fragile learning environment. Teachers must make every effort to establish and maintain learning spaces that are supportive and encouraging so that every child feels safe as music is shared and feedback is given.

Composition Requires a Different Kind of Teaching

Teaching composition is different from leading performance or teaching listening lessons. In both of those kinds of instruction, the teacher knows and often controls what the end result will be. It is the teacher who determines how pieces are supposed to sound or identifies the knowledge that students should acquire. In some cases, the teacher may be trying to elicit specific answers to questions or simply telling students information that they need to complete a task.

Creating something new is a little more chaotic than reproducing or describing something that already exists. The end product is not known when the composition lesson begins. This lack of a preconceived product requires teachers to trust their students and themselves as they engage in a process where learning emerges naturally.

The *Experiencing Music Composition* approach has its foundations in discovery learning and in the constructivist approach to learning. Springing from the work of Jerome Bruner,[1] Jean Piaget,[2] and John Dewey,[3] the central tenet of the approach involves engaging students in activities that pose authentic challenges within a specific domain. The students draw on their own experiences and prior knowledge as they consider how to address these challenges. Because students take the lead in defining problems, testing solutions, and making decisions about which actions to pursue, they become strongly invested in the learning process. This investment is integral to the achievement of compositional success. Similarly, the manner in which teachers approach tasks greatly influences student learning.

Like their students, most teachers know much more about music composition than they think they do. Teachers know what makes a singable melody, how to vary a motive, and how changing tone colors may alter the character of a musical idea. Creating lists of techniques and specifying how they should be applied may enable the crafting of a product, but it does so at the cost of student ownership and autonomy. However, these are necessary ingredients for individual artistry, creativity, and personal growth to emerge from their work.

Here are two teaching scenarios that illustrate why the teacher's approach matters.

Scenario 1: Ms. Yuto's First ABA Project

Ms. Yuto's class is about to present their small-group compositions. They have been asked to create pieces in ABA form that demonstrate contrasting dynamics, have two different melodies, and use dotted quarter notes followed by eighth notes somewhere in the piece. This is the new rhythm they have been working to master. Ms. Yuto provided the students with a rubric to serve as a guide for their composition and she is now ready to score each group's work. She records each performance for the students' portfolios as a way to document their work. As the performances take place, she notices a similarity to the pieces and a certain forced quality. Nearly all the pieces start with a loud A section and have a quiet B section. The dotted rhythms are used but seem to appear randomly in the melodies. When she asks the students about their pieces, they talk about how they included the required elements and who played what. Ms. Yuto wonders how she might help them create more expressive works. She had thought adding dynamics would accomplish that, but something still seems missing.

Scenario 2: Ms. Yuto's Revised ABA Project

Ms. Yuto's class has been listening to and performing pieces organized in ABA form. Believing that the group grasps the basic structure, Ms. Yuto invites the students to work in teams to create their own pieces. She distributes a *Sketchpage* with simple guidelines and lots of open space for students to write and sketch notations. She then coaches the groups to think about their pieces:

> Take a minute to think about the dotted quarter and eighth note rhythm. What does it feel like? Does it always create the same feeling? Does it feel differently when played on different instruments? What words would you use to describe the feeling? Discuss with your team which of these words will be the feelingful intention of your A and B sections. Note these ideas in the Feelingful Intention boxes.
>
> Next, consider which of the M.U.S.T.S. (she points to student-created posters labeled motion and stasis, unity and variety, sound and silence, tension and release, stability and instability are most important in bringing about the feelings that you have identified. Identify one or two principle pairs, the M.U.S.T.S., for the A and B sections and add these to the Musical Expressivity boxes on your *Sketchpage*.
>
> And finally, what musical ideas come to mind for rounding out the piece? Will your composition feature a single line or multiple lines? Which instruments

will be used in each section? How will the two sections relate to each other? Will they be similar or contrasting? Is there a compositional technique that will be important in your piece? As you make these and other decisions in inventing your piece, note them in the Artistic Craftsmanship boxes. This will help you tell us about your piece when you perform it.

When the students have finished crafting and rehearsing their pieces, Ms. Yuto listens to the performances. She is delighted to hear dotted rhythms that are crisp and martial as well as dotted rhythms that are gentle and lilting. She notes that students have contrasted their A and B sections in numerous ways. Teams have explored dynamics, instrumentation, major and minor, tempo, and more. As the composers introduce and perform their pieces, the class engages in discussions that reveal students' growing conceptions of music as an expressive and meaningful practice.

Working with "In-process" Composers

Sometimes it is difficult to trust that students will come up with ideas. However, the process of composing is quite similar to the experiences children have when they pursue creative writing. Given time and a little encouragement, they eventually find an idea and get under way. One particular challenge in music composition is that students often have musical ideas in their heads that they cannot articulate or perform. This is where the teacher can help by prompting students to think critically about what they are imagining.

Asking questions that evoke imaginative responses often helps students take a step toward getting started or advancing a germinal idea. For example, when students are creating a piece for their instruments, ask them to close their eyes and imagine themselves performing on stage while an audience sits and listens. Wait a few seconds and then add that everyone claps enthusiastically when the performance has ended. Ask the students to describe the piece they imagined.[4] Jot these thoughts down for the students or have them add them to their *Sketchpage*.

Another example of evoking imagination might be this: "Imagine that the creator of a video game has come to you and asked you to compose the music for her new mega-hit. The main character in the game is going to be 'Indu, the Ninja Cat.' How would the theme music for a ninja cat sound? How does it feel to be a ninja cat? How does a ninja cat move? What does it feel like to be in the situations that a ninja cat will be in? What is it like to be the character pursued by Indu? Can you hum or sing the music?"

The technique of using questions to prompt student action requires knowledge of the student and what might be blocking his or her creativity. Some students will simply state what their problem is, while others may have a hard time figuring it out. Some students have a very clear idea of what they want their music to sound like but cannot figure out how to make (or notate) the sounds. Other students are simply shy or hesitant to share their ideas. While these situations can be frustrating for student and teacher alike, they are temporary and will resolve with practice and supportive guidance. Let's consider two key points in the process when students are likely to get stuck and ask for help.

Idea Generation

Students often wonder where to begin their pieces. There is no correct answer for this question. The *Sketchpages* provided with each lesson present multiple entry points to each project. It is important to remember that every composer will find an individual entry point of comfort. For some composers, this will be a feeling or mood. Other composers may select an instrument or quickly discover a melodic or rhythmic fragment that sets the stage for the use of specific compositional techniques. Regardless of where and how the process starts, encourage students to think about the connections between all three capacities to enhance the overall quality of their work.

Idea Development or Extension

Once young composers have a work in progress, they may come to the teacher with questions about how a particular idea might evolve, or more directly, to ask what should come next. Be very careful in offering a response. It is easy to share solutions that are obvious to you as a "quick fix." It is more beneficial to the students to figure out the answer to the questions they have posed. When possible: Ask, don't tell.

Begin by asking to hear the piece and be prepared to listen more than once. Repeated listenings can be facilitated by saying, "I'm hearing a lot in this piece. May I hear it again so that I can get a better idea of what you are trying to do?" Once you have a clearer sense of what has been created, discuss the work with the composer using the following questions as appropriate:

- ♪ What should I know about your piece?
- ♪ Where did you begin?
- ♪ Was there a feeling, a particular M.U.S.T.S. pair that was appealing, or a technique that you are trying to use?
- ♪ How are you trying to capture that feeling?
- ♪ What are you doing to feature [insert M.U.S.T.S. pair named by the student]?
- ♪ How does the starting point capacity connect to the other capacities?
- ♪ Is there something specific that you are trying to do?
- ♪ What have you tried in an attempt to solve the current challenge?
- ♪ Are there other things you might try?
- ♪ Have you listened to any other composers who have worked with this genre, form, instrumentation, et cetera? What solutions did they use?
- ♪ Would you like me to offer a few options for you to try to see if they help you find what you are after?

As much as is possible, follow the student's lead in the discussion. Save the offer of presenting options as a final resort for times when students are truly at a loss for what to do. When presenting options, present at least three and make sure that composers know they do not have to use any of the presented options. The options are simply shared in hopes of spurring further exploration and idea trials to prompt student thinking.

Anchoring Knowledge, Inviting Inspiration

Another way to help students gain independence within the compositional process is to make a wide variety of resources available to them. Brief playlists organized by historical period, genre, style, compositional techniques, or other categorizations can provide auditory inspiration to composers facing specific challenges. Likewise, visual quick reference tools can serve to remind students of what they know or allow them to make important connections that further their work.

In the scenarios that appear in the opening of Section 3, Ms. Yuto gestured toward posters that her class might reference. These posters are called "Anchor Charts" and they can be created from student observations of how music works. As students listen to music, sing songs, or play instruments, they can be invited to notice and discuss compositional gestures. The techniques that they observe can then be recorded on posters, webpages, or other easily accessed locations, "anchoring" what has been learned for students to reference as they carry out their own compositional work.

While teachers can make and post resource charts, student-created charts constitute the most powerful learning tools because students feel a personal investment in the information represented. Each chart will be unique as it reflects what the students of a particular compositional community have discovered and analyzed together. Similarly, anchor charts do not have a set format. Rather, each chart evolves as teachers and students work together to document what they have discovered about a topic, tool, or idea. A quick Internet search for "music anchor chart" turns up a vast array of designs. Anchor charts may be focused on any capacity, may be organized by the M.U.S.T.S. (musical expressivities), or include definitions of key concepts, lists of ideas, or steps in process. The requirement common to all anchor charts is that they must be helpful to the students who will use them. An example of a completed anchor chart is shown in Figure 3.1.

MOTION	STASIS
❖ use short notes (8th notes)	❖ use long notes (half notes)
❖ have the pitch go up and down	❖ use pitches that repeat or stay close together
❖ use a galloping rhythm	❖ use boring rhythms
❖ use syncopation	❖ use a single instrument
❖ have lots of different instruments coming and going at different times	❖ use a slow tempo (adagio)
❖ use a fast tempo (presto!)	

Figure 3.1

Ways that composers use motion and stasis

Guidelines for Sharing Compositions—Giving and Receiving Feedback

Sharing compositions for feedback allows students the opportunity to improve their work while it is still in progress. It gives them direct insight as to how a particular audience may react and allows them to critically reflect on their own work and the work of others. As composers share music with each other, they discover new musical ideas, different ways of achieving particular outcomes, and compositional techniques that may be of use to them in the moment or in the future.

In addition to musical skills, composers develop enhanced communication skills as they speak about their work. They also learn to offer specific praise and appropriate critique to their peers. As their experiences with composition and presentation grow, they gain confidence in their ability describe their intentions. They become increasingly able to discuss their working processes and they recognize the ongoing development of their compositional capacities. To foster this growth, teachers must create and maintain an environment that allows students to feel safe in sharing work that is often highly personal. The best way to do this is through a direct partnership with students.

Setting Expectations and Creating Guidelines

Before students can offer feedback on the compositions of their peers, they need an opportunity to think about how they will feel as they receive comments. Teachers can invite students to imagine sharing a composition with their classmates and prompt them to think about the type of feedback that they would hope to receive. Students should also consider how they would like comments made.

Begin with a composition model created by the teacher or a student who is not in the class. Have students practice offering praise and constructive feedback. Use the statements made by the students as examples to put together a list of guidelines, such as those shown in Figure 3.2, to help students provide useful feedback in a pleasant and supportive manner.

Figure 3.2

Tips for composers offering feedback

- Be kind and give the type of feedback that you would hope to receive.
- Offer praise.
- Critique the composition; do not criticize the composer (performer).
- Be specific in your feedback so that the composer knows exactly what you are talking about.
- Talk about what the composer asked listeners to comment on.
- Speak from your own perspective using phrases such as:
  - I think _____ worked for me because _____.
  - The use of _____ made me feel _____.
  - As I listened to your piece, I learned that_____.
  - I'm wondering if you tried _____ ? I ask because _____.
  - Maybe you could try _____ because it _____.
  - I'm curious about _____· Can you tell us why _____?

It is also important for composers to think about how they will accept feedback. It can be difficult to listen to what others have to say about work that you are deeply connected to and perhaps quite proud of. However, composers benefit from experiences that require them to gain some objective distance from their music so they can thoughtfully evaluate what is working and what may need further work. Figure 3.3 outlines a few thoughts that composers should keep in mind as they listen to feedback.

> - Listen. Just listen. Do not attempt to justify your approach. Simply pay attention to how others are reacting and responding to your work so that you can decide if you wish to change anything or continue on the path you have pursued so far.
> - Be open to ideas that don't immediately make sense to you. New listeners hear differently than you do.
> - Suggestions are only suggestions. You do not have to change your music to address every suggestion that is offered.
> - Listen to praise. It highlights your best work and points out the skills that you have and can use to improve your piece.

Figure 3.3

Tips for composers receiving feedback

Composers' Circles

Composers' Circles are gatherings of composers, teachers, performers, and others who may provide useful feedback on compositions in progress or completed works. Circles often involve whole classes when composition projects have been completed in small groups, but they may also be limited in size with just three to five composers who listen to each other's work and offer constructive commentary.

It is important that teachers facilitate initial Composers' Circles so that students learn how to fill the roles of presenter and responder. Circles typically begin with a composer, or group of composers, introducing a piece. The composer should be encouraged to share any information that may be relevant to the listeners. This may include information about inspiration, feelingful intentions, musical expressivities, techniques being used, or problems that the composer is seeking to address. Figure 3.4 shows some statements that may help young composers introduce their work.

> - The piece that I am working on is called _____.
> - I am trying to create the feeling of _____.
> - I have used (M.U.S.T.S) to try to invite a feeling of _____.
> - The first musical idea that I tried _____.
> - I have tried using (technique) to _____, but I am finding that_____.
> - I know I need to work on _____.
> - I am hoping that someone might have a suggestion for how I could_____.
> - I am open to any reaction.
> - Please tell me *what* you think works and *why* you think it works for you.

Figure 3.4

Following the composer's lead

Once the introduction has been given and the audience has heard the work, the teacher should encourage students to offer constructive criticisms. It is helpful to invite praise and criticism in balance: two praise comments to each comment of constructive criticism. As students become comfortable with this process and gain confidence as composers, the balance of comments may be adjusted to suit the needs of each composer as is shown in the written comment form of Figure 3.5.

Figure 3.5

COMPOSER FEEDBACK

Title _____

Composer(s) _____

CRITIC 1:		CRITIC 2:		CRITIC 3:	
	 An idea to consider				
	 An idea to consider				

Revision ideas from feedback:

Working with Reluctant Sharers

Unfortunately, some young composers may be very reluctant to share what they have created. They may not even want to share their composition with friends or the teacher. In such cases, it is important to respect the young composer's reluctance while continuing to show interest in what he or she is doing.

Composers who do not receive feedback on their work are unlikely to further develop their compositional capacities. Therefore, it is important to find ways to provide feedback to reluctant sharers as soon as possible. Some students will agree to participate in one-on-one conferences, either with the teacher or a friend within the class. Others will be comfortable with recording their compositions so that the teacher can listen to them apart from the student with feedback taking written form. In this situation, written feedback in early interactions must offer valid praise with only a few minor criticisms. This will help students overcome the fear of criticism while allowing some productive feedback to be given.

As trust grows, students can be gently led into participation in a Circle. Interaction should begin with reluctant sharers being invited to offer suggestions but not expected to share their work. By participating in this way, their confidence may grow and they may begin to feel emotionally safe within the group. Once trust has been established, reluctant sharers may become more willing to present their music for feedback.

Putting Feedback to Good Use

The feedback that composers receive from the teacher or peers within the Composers' Circles holds varying potential. Composers often put the ideas presented to them to immediate use if they are working on a composition that is still in progress, but they are far less likely to apply suggestions to a finished work.

Encouraging students to revise work that they consider completed requires a cautious approach. Educational researcher Sandra Stauffer has suggested that students do not spontaneously revise their works until sometime around age 11.[5] Prior to that, when the child has completed the piece, he or she is finished with it and ready to move on to the next thing. Mentors can make suggestions like "I think there is potential for this to be a longer piece. Do you think there might be another part to it?" or "You have created a lovely song. I wonder if it might be the chorus of a longer piece." However, young composers may not agree and may wish to start a new work. It is important to respect their developmental stage while continuing to suggest ways revision might work. Students may be more open to suggestions for revisions if those suggestions further their own artistic intentions.

Post-Performance Reflections

As students share the final versions of their pieces, teachers should facilitate questioning that reveals multiple feelingful intentions, each of the musical expressivities, and the tools and techniques of artistic craftsmanship. Multiple capacities unfold in every piece. Taking time to identify them and discuss how they work reveals music's complex constructions and potentials for expressive artistry.

Moreover, some children will discover new things about their own compositions as they describe them and as they hear the observations made by those who have listened to their work. Other children will recognize their own techniques and processes only when they hear similar ones described by their peers. Allowing the processes of composition to be experienced, observed, and discussed presents multiple entry points for young composers to learn more about themselves and the art of composition.

Making the Most of Limited Timeframes

In the ever-present battle against the clock, class time is seldom given to the creation and sharing of compositions. Yet considerable learning occurs when students analyze and discuss what they have observed in the composition of others. In just 2–3 minutes, pairs of students can identify and draw connections between the feelingful intentions, musical expressivities, and the techniques of artistic craftsmanship used within a short piece. In just 3–5 minutes, small groups of students can describe how the choice of feelingful intentions and use of compositional techniques were designed to engage a particular audience or bring about a specific type of reaction. Brief and focused analysis and discussion helps student hone their skills of perception so that they become increasingly aware of the tools and techniques available to them as they work to artistically craft music for expressive purposes. This is time well invested.

Notes

1 Bruner, J. S. (1961). The act of discovery. *Harvard Educational Review*, 31(1): 21–32.
2 Piaget, J. (1936). *Origins of intelligence in the child*. London: Routledge & Kegan Paul.
3 Dewey, J. (1938). *Experience and education*. New York, NY: Kappa Delta Pi.
4 Deutsch, D. (2012). Teaching gifted learners in composition. In M. Kaschub & J. Smith (Eds.), *Composing our future: Preparing music educators to teach composition* (p. 136). New York, NY: Oxford University Press.
5 Stauffer, S. L. (1998, April). *Children as composers: Changes over time*. Paper presented at the biennial convention of the Music Educators National Conference, Phoenix, AZ.

4
Teacher Guides and Student *Sketchpages*

Teacher Guides

This section contains 15 teacher guides designed to help teachers mentor upper elementary students as they explore composition. Each guide includes

1. an overview of a composition project;
2. descriptions of how to facilitate student learning throughout the compositional process;
3. examples of questions that can be used to prompt the development of compositional capacities; and
4. one or more *Sketchpages* for students to use as they create original compositions within each project.

Curricular Organization & Compositional Strands

Projects are organized by suggested grade level across the five different compositional genres. Throughout each strand, young composers will consider the feelingful intentions, the musical expressivities, and the tools and techniques of artistic craftsmanship that suit a particular genre and project. They also will explore their creative potential as composers and come to value their own interpretations and understandings of what makes their music artful and important.

	Songwriting & Choral Music	Composition & Visual Media	Instrumental Music	Electronic Music & Digital Media	Music Theatre
Gr.3	Seasons: A Song Cycle in Four Movements	Composing for Adventuresome Characters	Sounds & Notations	Duets with Tone Matrix Generators	Getting to Know Me: Introducing Character Songs
Gr.4	Tonic & Dominant Friendship Songs	Before & After	Percussion Canon	Head in the Game	There's More than One Way to Tell a Story
Gr.5	Our Blues Album	From Silent Movie to Film Score: Just "Say Cheese"	Soundscapes: A Walk through the Fair	Podcasts with Peer Composers	Mini-Musical: A Story in Just Five Songs

Songwriting and Choral Music

The creation of songs is often one of the first compositional activities that children pursue. As the voice tends to be the primary instrument of young composers, song is a natural outlet for musical thinking. Songs also lend themselves to the structure of stories—another creative medium that children warmly embrace. The three lesson projects featured in this book invite young composers to think about the seasons of the year, the give and take of friendships (through a little tonic and dominant harmonic interplay), and exploring emotion as it relates to troublesome events while they revel in the Blues.

Composition and Visual Media

Music often plays a supportive, yet critical, role in how we experience stories. In the composition and visual media strand of the *Experiencing Music Composition* curriculum, students undertake three projects involving the creation of music: 1) for a single story-book character traveling through multiple locations; 2) exploring the emotional impact of change related to before and after photos; and 3) a score for a short movie.

Instrumental Music

For composers who wish to create music involving more than one performer, the need for some formal system of sharing musical ideas soon arises. The first project of the instrumental strand allows teachers to create a "need" for notation. To bring notation into regular use, the second project engages students in the creation of percussion canon in an activity where notation is used in a limited and purposeful manner to maintain student creativity. In the final project, students collaborate in small-group composition within the context of a whole class project to capture the experience of walking though fairgrounds and passing multiple attractions with unique and interesting musical implications.

Electronic Music and Digital Media

Electronic music and digital media are highly accessible to young musicians, yet the physicality of making sound with the body is still a critical experience as children grow and develop an understanding of music. The activities in this strand blend technology with acoustic music-making to capitalize on the appeal of digital formats while preserving the experiential physicality of music making. From partnering acoustic instruments (perfect for recorders or beginning band or orchestra players) with tone generators to student-defined compositions that become integral parts of podcasts, students will learn how composers create and promote their music in the digital age.

Music Theater

Whether it is live theater or theater by way of Hollywood film, music theater is a genre that captures young people's imaginations. The interplay of quirky characters with classic themes and great music is nearly irresistible. In this strand, composers will begin by exploring how a fairy tale might become a song, how a prop or minor character might view the major characters or some particular event within the story, and then collaborate as a class to create a mini-musical featuring five different types of Broadway-styled songs to bring a story to life—or to a theatrical stage.

45

Projects for Grade 3

SEASONS
A Song Cycle in Four Movements

Composition Strand - Songwriting and choral music

About This Project

Many artists have chosen to create music, visual art or choreographed dance to capture some aspect of the four seasons. In this project, or series of projects, young composers are invited to explore the differences between the seasons as well as the contrasts that may exist within a single season.

This project may be approached as a

- teacher-facilitated whole class composition for the current season. This will allow the lesson to be used four times each year.
- small-group composition with each small group creating its own version of the current season. This will allow the lesson to be used four times each year.
- small-group composition with each small group adopting a different season. This format would likely be used just once in a year. It could also be done in fall and again in late spring to see how the composers have grown over the course of the year.

The whole group configuration is most appropriate for students who have little to no previous experience with songwriting. For students who have engaged in whole class songwriting in grades K-2, small-group composition can be very successful.

Materials

- *Sketchpages* for the season(s) being composed
- Classroom instruments; found sounds may also be used to enhance the sense of a particular season

Project Time

- It will take approximately 45 minutes to complete the introduction, composing, sharing, and closing discussion portions of the lesson for each season. Much depends on how long it takes to create the lyrics.

Discussion Questions to Develop Compositional Capacities

- Feelingful Intention—What feelings are associated with this season? Are there contrasting feelings associated with it?
- Musical Expressivity—Which of the M.U.S.T.S. might most effectively enhance the feelings we have identified? For example, how might tension and release play a role in the cold of winter or the heat of summer?
- Artistic Craftsmanship—How do the lyrics partner with the music? Are specific compositional techniques used to highlight words or ideas within the text?

Sequence of Activities

- Open the project with the whole class. Brainstorm ideas about one season. Prompt student thinking by asking: How does the season feel? What do people do in this season and how do they feel while they are doing it? What contrasting ideas are there? (i.e., winter: fun playing in snow, but icy cold winds and slippery conditions; spring rain and mud, but flowers and warmer days, etc.) Generate a long list of possibilities for the season and display it where students can easily reference it as they work. Point out to the students that they may use these or similar descriptors as they make notes in the Feelingful Intention part of *Sketchpage*.
- If students are moving into small-group work, take a moment to review how they might create text, explore, test and select musical ideas. Distribute the *Sketchpages* for the season(s) being composed and remind students of how much time they have to work, which instruments are available, and any other expectations.
- If students are continuing as a whole class, categorize the ideas that students have offered. These ideas then serve as a starting point for creating verses. For example, all descriptors of outdoor play may be grouped together. Students should be encouraged to add these descriptive words and phrases to their *Sketchpages* as the teacher adds them to a projected *Sketchpage* that everyone can see. Note: Please visit www.oup.com/us/experiencingmusiccompositioningrades3to5 for full color images. This helps students learn to use the *Sketchpage* as an organizer.

- Create the text with students.
  - Using the words, ideas, and phrases that have been grouped together, ask students to make up a first line to introduce the topic. If the line needs to fit within a particular metrical space, i.e., 8 beats, then snap out 8 beats.
  - Have one student speak a line, in rhythm if possible. Have the class echo-chant the idea. Gather a minimum of three ideas and more if students have them. Display all suggestions where they can be seen. Words-only may be a sufficient memory aid, but if your students are familiar with stem notation, it may be added to indicate rhythm. Ideas are often reordered or revised as the process unfolds. Label the ideas with shapes for easy reference. Do not use numbers or student names as these imply priority and ownership.
  - Once two to three ideas have emerged, ask the students if anyone can think of a second line for any of the clustered ideas. Repeat the process above.
  - At this point, one idea may become a clear front runner. If not, have the class vote on which idea they would like to pursue. Ideas that were not chosen should be saved in a format where they can be revisited and used at another time.
  - Continue the process for lines three and four. Lines 1 and 2 may even become lines 3 and 4 as new lines are created. Encourage flexibility and openness as musical and textual ideas often shift places as composers work.
- Encourage students to link expressive ideas to the text. Students may address one or more of the M.U.S.T.S. For example, are there verses that will have faster or slower tempos (more motion or more stasis)? Will any particular sound be used throughout the song (to create unity) or will any sounds be added to some sections, but not others (to create variety)? Students may make note of these ideas in and around the text on their *Sketchpage* as the teacher adds them to the projected *Sketchpage*.
- Coach students the creation of a melody.
  - Invite students to read the text aloud. Encourage them speak expressively and note the rise and fall of their voices.
  - Ask students if anyone has a way to sing one of the lines of the text. If no one volunteers, introduce the "Minute Maker." For one minute everyone in the room sings ideas softly, trying as many ideas as they can, repeating the ones they like. The teacher does this, too, but very softly and while looking very thoughtful! At the end of one minute, ask for volunteers or ask if anyone heard any ideas that the group should consider. Invite the composer to sing the idea and the class to echo it.
  - Continue, using the same process that was used for text generation above.
  - As each idea is shared, discuss its effectiveness in sonifying—shaping sound to match the feelingful experience—of the season. Students working in small groups should record their ideas or sing them

repeatedly and notate them in any way that will help them to remember what they have made up.

- When the class or small groups have created both text and melody, record a performance of the song.

- Invite students to listen to the recording and identify things that work and things that could be done to improve the composition. Should other sounds be added? Sounds omitted? Is greater dynamic contrast needed? Does the text have good flow? Are there any surprises or instances of variety that help the audience stay interested in the piece? If students know what they want, but are unsure of how to achieve it, take a moment to explain the craftsmanship technique they need to know.

- Allow students to make adjustments, test, record and listen again as time permits. These steps help students learn the process of critical evaluation and revision. Remember to make a final recording that can be shared with classroom teachers, parents and students.

- As you listen to student work, formulate questions that will help students identify affective compositional practices. Questions, such as the following, should be tied to the specific compositional work completed by the students:

  ○ What did you hear that was really interesting to you? Why was it so interesting?
  ○ Which of the M.U.S.T.S. seemed most important at that point? Why?
  ○ What you just described gave the piece unity. How does that sound hold the piece together?
  ○ What role did text play in the work? Would the piece be as effective if the text was removed or if the text for another season were substituted? Why or why not?

- Connect the students' experience of composing to works by other composers. Examples are offered below under "Optional Extensions."

Optional Extensions

Play and discuss examples from various styles of songs about seasons. Which seem to best sonify a feeling about the season? Why?

Models for Listening Analysis

- *Winter Wonderland,* by Felix Bernard
- "Stopping by Woods on a Snowy Evening" from *Frostiana,* by Randall Thompson
- *When Fall Comes to New England,* by Cheryl Wheeler
- *The Burning Tree,* by Different Shoes
- *Autumn in New York,* by Ella Fitzgerald and Louis Armstrong
- "Summertime" from *Porgy and Bess,* by George Gershwin
- *Summer Song,* by Chad and Jeremy

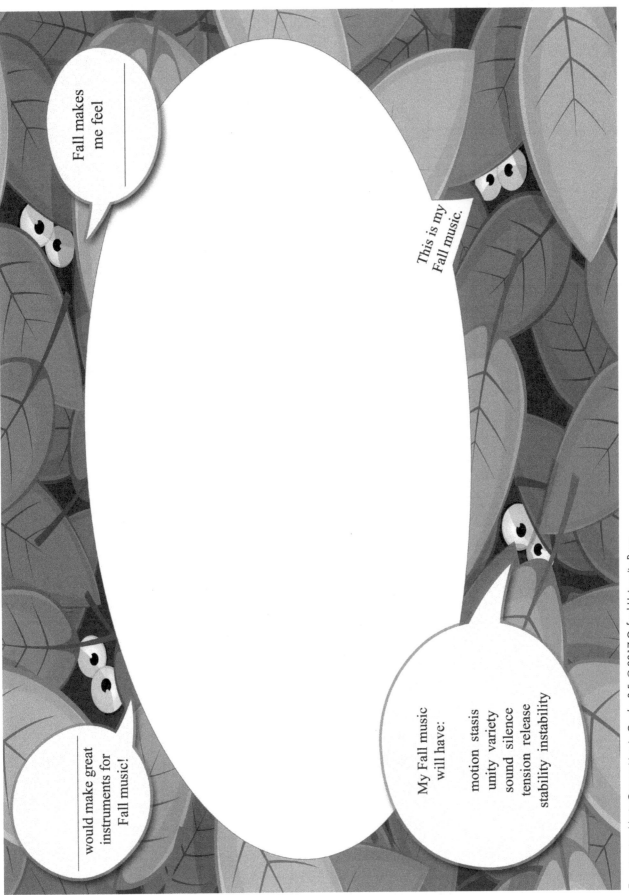

54

Experiencing Music Composition in Grades 3-5, © 2017 Oxford University Press

56

Summer makes
me feel _____

My Summer music will have
(circle your choices):
motion stasis unity variety
sound silence tension release
stability instability

My music goes like this ⇧

_____ would make great
instruments for
Summer music!

COMPOSING FOR ADVENTURESOME CHARACTERS

Composition Strand - Composition and visual media

About This Project

Louise, the Adventures of a Chicken is a delightful children's picture book by Kate DiCamillo and Harry Bliss (HarperCollins, 2008). The story focuses on Louise as she seeks excitement and adventure by traveling to three exotic locales. In each chapter of her chronicled adventures, Louise encounters challenging situations and robust characters that frame moments of self-discovery and eventually draw Louise back home to the farm.

As a chicken appearing in four vivid settings, Louise is a character clearly in need of a theme to ground her. This lesson begins with the whole class composing just such a theme for Louise. Students then work in small groups to situate this theme in one of the four settings (pirate ship, circus, bazaar, or farm) explored in the book.

Materials

- A *Sketchpage* for each group
- Pitched and unpitched classroom instruments
- One copy DiCamillo's *Louise, the Adventures of a Chicken* (Note: It is helpful to give each group a copy of the story book, but a single copy can be shared)
- Invented, transitional, or traditional notation paper may be copied onto the "B-side" of the *Sketchpage* or made available for students to select as needed

Project Time

- This lesson will fully occupy a 45-minute class period.

Discussion Questions to Develop Compositional Capacities

- Feelingful Intention—What is the overall feeling that suits an adventuresome chicken? How does that feeling change when Louise is in a specific setting?

- Musical Expressivity—Which of the M.U.S.T.S. is most useful in altering the theme to fit the particular settings within the story? Are any of the M.U.S.T.S. more prominent than others in maintaining the feeling of "adventure"? Why or why not?
- Artistic Craftsmanship—What compositional techniques did each group use to vary the theme? How did the technique help the listener understand what it was like to be Louise in a particular part of the story?

58

Sequence of Activities

Working Together as a Whole Class

- Ask the students if they know any cartoon characters with their own special music. Ask students to describe the character and how their music sounds. For example, Superman's music is heroic and the music begins with a big leap as he takes to the sky.
- Once you have a few examples, introduce the term "theme" and explain how a theme describes a character with sounds instead of words.
- Introduce the idea of composing music to enhance the telling of a story. Have students listen as you read the story. Encourage them to think about words they would use to describe Louise.
- Write the students' descriptive words on the board. To extend the development of intentional capacity, ask the students if the descriptions they offered apply to Louise throughout the whole story or in some parts of the story more than others. Circle the "whole story" answers and note where other words applied (pirate ship, circus, bazaar, or farm).
- Working as a whole class, create Louise's theme. Ask the students to think about the list of descriptive words and sounds they have generated. Invite the students to close their eyes and imagine Louise's theme.
- Ask the students to perform their ideas. The class should echo each idea so that every student internalizes how the music feels. Name these ideas on the board as the "skipping" idea, the "hero" idea, etc.
- Once all ideas are posted, have the class discuss the strengths of each idea and consider minor adjustments, mergers, and revisions. Generally one or two ideas will emerge as class favorites. If necessary, vote to select the strongest idea, emphasizing that there were many good ideas, but that just one is needed for this particular project.
- Sing the chosen Louise's theme several times so that everyone knows it well.
- Discuss the term "variation." Ask students to offer ideas about things that can change in a piece of music (rhythm, pitch, dynamics, instruments, tempo, etc.). Place answers on the board so that students can refer to this list as they work.

Small-Group Work

- Divide the class into small groups and assign each group a section of the story (pirate ship, circus, bazaar, or farm). Ask each group to create a list of descriptive words that apply to Louise in their assigned setting. Give the students 2–3 minutes to work. Remind them to add these words to the Feelingful Intention space on their *Sketchpages*.

- Ask the students to match sounds to their descriptive words. Prompt questions might include these:
  - What does the theme sound like when Louise is on the pirate ship during rough seas?
  - What might the theme sound like when Louise teeters on the high wire?
  - How might the theme change when Louise is captured and caged with other chickens?
  - What does the theme sound like when Louise finally settles back on the farm?

- Once this is done, encourage the students to select one M.U.S.T.S. area that seems to fit their part of the story and at least two variation techniques that they can apply to create their variations on Louise's theme. Encourage students to note these ideas on their *Sketchpages*.

- Invite students to collect whatever instruments and other tools they need to complete their work.

- Allow 10 minutes of work time. Remember, it is easy to grant an extra 2 or 3 minutes of work time, but difficult to take it away.

Putting It All Together

- Performance and Refinement: Discuss the performance order with the students. It is easy to create an introduction by having all the students perform the original version of Louise's theme. As it concludes, the music for the pirate part of the story should begin. The composers of the pirate and circus sections should quickly discuss when the music of the circus part should begin. Similar conversations are needed between "circus and bazaar" and "bazaar and farm" composing teams.

- Student Reflection: After the initial performance, discuss how each variation worked. What was interesting about the music of each section? What techniques did the composers use to capture the essence of the adventure in their part of the story? Which of the M.U.S.T.S. was most useful?

- Opportunity for Revision: Give the students one minute to discuss with their team how they might make their section of the music work better. Perform again. Ask students to identify the changes they made and how they think the change impacted the music.

60

I once met a chicken named Louise.
She just loved to travel. Yes, yes she did.
She said she felt _____ whenever she was on an
adventure. One time, she was [with pirates, at a circus, visiting a bazaar,
back at this farm] and she said it felt _____. I always
thought that music full of [motion-stasis, unity-variety, sound-silence,
tension-release, stability-instability] should have been playing as she described what
happened on that trip. Just imagine how (two variation techniques) _____
and _____ could have brought that story to life!
Can you hear it? Well, you go right ahead.
Draw the music that you imagine fitting that adventure
in this space, right here, just in front of me.
I'm looking forward to seeing it...

SOUNDS AND NOTATIONS

Composition Strand - Instrumental music

About This Project

It is important for young composers to learn how to use traditional notation. This lesson is designed to create a "need to know" experience that will help students discover the value of a commonly understood notational system. Pieces are composed by one group of students but performed by another. The performances tend to lack faithfulness to the original composers' ideas. Consequently, the importance of sharing a common symbol system to communicate musical ideas becomes apparent. This sets the stage for the introduction of formal notation.

Materials

- *Sketchpage* with separate invented notation paper
- Pitched and unpitched instruments (small percussion, recorders, Orff instruments, etc.)

Project Time

- It will take approximately 45 minutes to complete this project.

Discussion Questions to Develop Compositional Capacities

Feelingful Intention, Musical Expressivity, and Artistic Craftsmanship are fully determined by students in this activity. Students should be reminded to consider each capacity as they compose and to be ready to describe their choices and decisions after their work is performed.

Sequence of Activities

The Composition Task

- Review the task guidelines section of the *Sketchpage* with the class.

- Direct composition groups to locations that separate them from each other so that they cannot easily hear what other groups are composing. Encourage groups to work very quietly and to keep their compositions "secret."

- When the compositions are complete, collect the *Sketchpages* from students. Leave the invented scores with the instruments.

Interpreted Performances

- Guide each team of students to the instruments and score of a group as distant from their first workspace as possible.

- Give performers 3–4 minutes to figure out their interpretation of the new scores.

- Invite each group to perform. Have the composers rate the accuracy of the performer's reading of the score. Use a 10-point scale with "10" equaling "totally what we wanted" and "1" representing "not at all what we wanted." Most performances will be rated in the middle of the scale.

- Initiate a discussion of how a shared system of notation can help composers and performers communicate when they are not able to speak with one another.

Intended Performance and Reflection

- Have students return to their original composition workspaces and redistribute *Sketchpages* among them.

- Invite each composition group to perform their own pieces as they were intended to sound.

- Discuss the use of compositional capacities and whether those capacities were present in the first performance of their work. This reinforces the importance of beginning to learn and use a standardized approach to notation in future compositions.

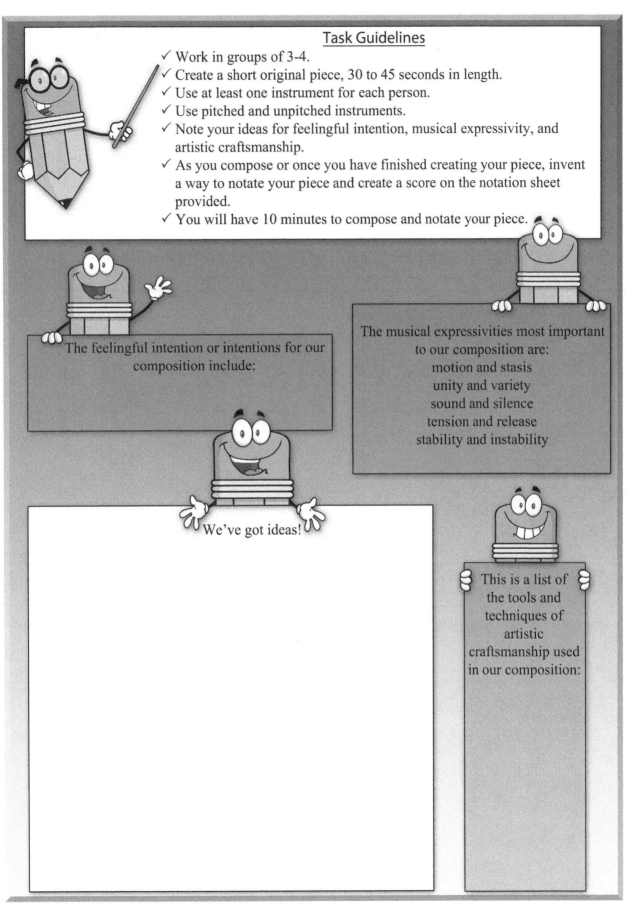

Task Guidelines

✓ Work in groups of 3-4.
✓ Create a short original piece, 30 to 45 seconds in length.
✓ Use at least one instrument for each person.
✓ Use pitched and unpitched instruments.
✓ Note your ideas for feelingful intention, musical expressivity, and artistic craftsmanship.
✓ As you compose or once you have finished creating your piece, invent a way to notate your piece and create a score on the notation sheet provided.
✓ You will have 10 minutes to compose and notate your piece.

63

The feelingful intention or intentions for our composition include:

The musical expressivities most important to our composition are:
motion and stasis
unity and variety
sound and silence
tension and release
stability and instability

We've got ideas!

This is a list of the tools and techniques of artistic craftsmanship used in our composition:

DUETS WITH TONE MATRIX GENERATORS

Composition Strand - Electronic music and digital media

About This Project

This lesson is designed to challenge young composers to move beyond single line compositions to explore biphonic texture. The composition activity partners an acoustic instrument with a generator. Ideally, the composer is familiar with the acoustic instrument and can play it comfortably. The new tool added in this lesson is the tone matrix generator (TMG). The TMG will be used to create a simple accompaniment figure over which the acoustic melody will be played.

The lesson may be approached with a single composer creating the lines for both the TMG and the acoustic instrument, or composers may work in pairs with one responsible for each part. While some teams may actively share the simultaneous creation of both lines, most will create an accompaniment figure and then add a melody to it. At the end of the project, students can be invited to discuss how they approached the task and what seemed to work best for them as a way of expanding their understanding of possible compositional processes.

Materials

- A *Sketchpage* for each student or pair of students
- A melodic instrument that the composer is comfortable playing
- Access to a tone matrix generator. There are many tone matrix generation tools that are quickly grasped by young learners. For example, http://www.tonematrix.audiotool.com is a free, easy-to-use, web-based generator. Similarly, CandyCaneApps offers *Melodica* and Loftlab offers *TonePad* for a variety of smart device platforms.

Project Time

- This activity requires approximately 30 minutes.

Discussion Questions to Develop Compositional Capacities

- Feelingful Intention—What mood, character or feeling could you explore with two instruments? Is it possible to create a single feelingful impression with the tone generator and instrument that you have chosen? Do two instruments require two feelings?
- Musical Expressivity—Which of the M.U.S.T.S. will work best with the tone generator and instrument you have chosen to bring about that mood, character, or feeling in sound? Are different expressive pairs needed for the tone generator and the acoustic instrument?
- Artistic Craftsmanship—How will the tone generator and the acoustic instrument interact? Will they take turns, as if in a conversation? Will both instruments play all the time? Will one instrument play all the time while the other plays only some of the time?

Sequence of Activities

Thinking about Artistic Craftsmanship

- Open the lesson by asking students to identify what they think composers can do with two instruments that might be impossible or harder to do with just one instrument.
- Describe today's project to the students: *"Today we will make up pieces for two parts: an acoustic melody and an electronically generated accompaniment. Can you begin to imagine how that might sound? What are some of the ways we can use two instruments to create music?"* Create a list of the answers and display it where the students can see it as they compose.
- Demonstrate how the tone matrix generator works. Invite a student to create a loop and discuss the feeling that loop creates for the listeners. Discuss compositional possibilities. *"If another instrument were added, what might it play?"* Briefly demonstrate an acoustic melody played along with the loop.
- Determine whether the students are working individually, in pairs, or if they may choose either configuration. Invite partners to sit together.

Considering Feelingful Intention and Musical Expressivity

- Distribute copies of the *Sketchpage* for this activity; "B-side" notation paper is not needed for this project.

- Have students select an acoustic instrument and write its name in the speech bubble that reads "My duet partner is the _____."
- Invite students to consider what mood, character, or feeling they would like to explore in their composition. Encourage students to make note of this thought on the *Sketchpage*. If the TMG and the acoustic instrument will create different impressions, note different feeling intentions for each instrument.
- Composers should also decide which of the M.U.S.T.S. will be most important in capturing the mood, character, or feeling they are trying to achieve. This, too, should be noted on the *Sketchpage*.
- Provide 8–10 minutes for students to compose their pieces. Remind students that their intentions may change as they compose and that the evolution of musical ideas is common. Encourage them to note these changes on their *Sketchpage*.

Performance and Refinement

- Invite individual composers or partnered composers to perform their composition. Ask the students to say just a few words of introduction addressing what they hope the audience will find interesting in their piece. Charge the audience with trying to figure out how the composer(s) used the TMG and the acoustic instrument to create the "interesting idea" that the composer identified.

Student Reflection

- After students have shared their duets it is possible to discuss the pros and cons of tone matrix generators as tools for composition. What are the advantages to working with tone generators and what are the limitations? If students could design a tone generator to suit their needs, what would it be able to do?
- At this point teachers may wish to explore applications and software that allow for the creation of more complex tone matrices and loops.

68

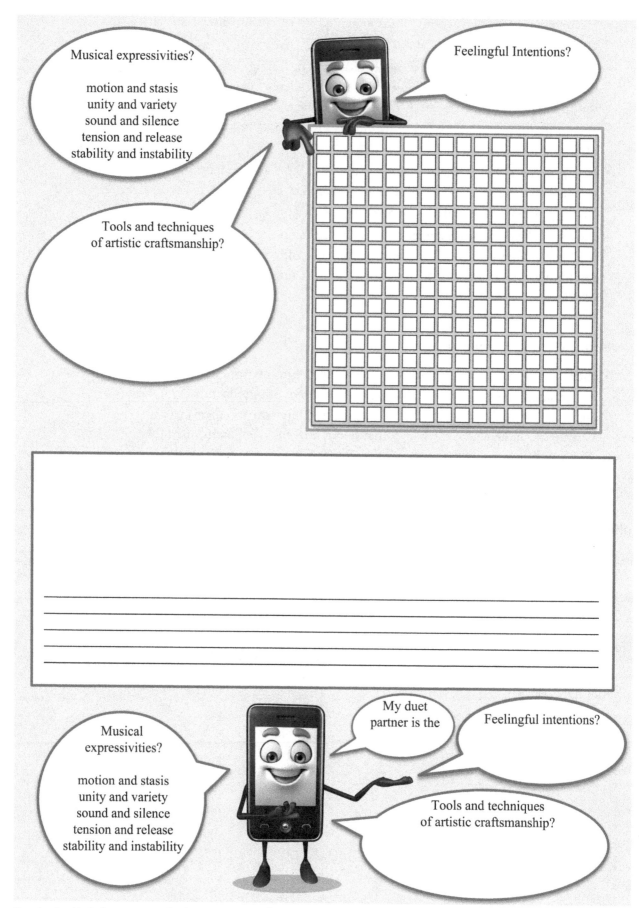

GETTING TO KNOW ME
Introducing Character Songs

Composition Strand - Music theater

About This Project

In this lesson students will learn how to create an "I am" song. "I am" songs are most commonly sung by the main character in a musical and are meant to introduce a character to an audience. These songs often have an ABA form in which each section serves a particular purpose:

- The "A" section is the verse and presents the main tune of the song. The song lyrics tell the audience something about the main character's current situation. This section is sometimes repeated with different lyrics when a longer song is desired or more information needs to be shared with the audience to advance the story.
- Section "B" sharply contrasts with "A." It serves to highlight the character's dream or vision.
- The "A" section returns with lyrics that reveal what the character hopes will be his or her future self. Slight changes are made to the music to boost dramatic impact and bring the song to a big finish.

Materials

- *Sketchpage;* no B-side is needed as the teacher transcribes this song or icons are drawn around written lyrics
- A fairy tale or story that the children know well
- Classroom instruments

Project Time

- This lesson can be divided into three sessions:
    1. analytical listening and lyric writing, approximately 30 minutes

2. melodic composition, approximately 20 minutes
3. compositional enhancement, performance, and discussion, approximately 20 minutes

Discussion Questions to Develop Compositional Capacities

- Feelingful Intention—How does this character feel about himself or herself? What are his or her dreams and what feelings do those dreams inspire?
- Musical Expressivity—Which of the M.U.S.T.S. best suit the unique personality traits of the character and help convey the character's message and feelings to the listener?
- Artistic Craftsmanship—How is the contrast between the A and B sections of the piece achieved? What tools or techniques can composers use to capture the hopes and dreams offered in the B section?

Sequence of Activities

Session 1—Analytical Listening and Lyric Writing

- It is important for young composers to hear and analyze compositions similar to those they are trying to create. Begin the compositional process for creating an "I am" song by analyzing existing songs of this genre. Two possibilities from classic and recent musicals are "I Feel Pretty" from *West Side Story* and "I'm a Believer" from *Shrek*. Discuss what happens in each song. What does the main character sing about? How does the music make the audience feel about the character? What tools or techniques did the composer use to help the audience experience these feelings?

- Using the students' observations, discuss the three sections of the "I am" song.

- With the class, select a character to feature in a class-composed "I am" song. Ideal characters are those who are familiar to the students. Consider characters from fairy tales and short stories. Try to avoid characters that have a pre-existing theme; it will be tempting for students to overly rely on these ideas as they work. Project the *Sketchpage* and add the character's name.

- Encourage the children to imagine being the character. What would they want the audience to know? For example, drawing on E. B. White's *Charlotte's Web* and assuming the role of "Wilbur," the opening section might have lyrics like this:

> *I am a pig and I sit all alone,*
> *I wish had a friend of my own.*
> *Although I'm surrounded by mud and hay*
> *I just want a friend to come and play.*

- Work through the song planner, discussing the ABA section and making notes about the character.

- Using the notes added to the planner, begin to create song lyrics.
  - Work with just one section of the song at a time to minimize confusion.
  - Invite everyone to make up a first line. If the line needs to fit within a particular metrical space, i.e., 8 beats, then snap 8 beats.
  - Have one student speak his or her idea in rhythm, if possible. Have the class echo-chant the idea. Gather a minimum of three ideas and more if students have them. Display all suggestions where they can be seen. The words alone may be a sufficient memory aid, but if students are familiar with stem notation, it may be added to the text to indicate rhythm. Ideas are often reordered or revised as the process unfolds. Label the ideas with shapes for easy reference. Do not use numbers or student names as these imply priority and ownership.
  - Once a few ideas have emerged, ask the students if anyone can think of a second line. Repeat the process above.
  - At this point, one idea may become a clear front runner. If not, have the class vote on which idea they would like to pursue. Ideas that were not chosen should be saved in a format where they can be revisited and used at another time.
  - Continue the process for lines 3 and 4. Lines 1 and 2 may even become lines 3 and 4 as new lines are created. Encourage flexibility and openness as musical and textual ideas often shift places as composers work.
  - When verse 1 is complete, add the text to the "Lyrics" section of the *Sketchpage*.
- Repeat this process for the contrasting "B" section and the return of the "A" section.

Session 2—Composition, Performance, and Discussion

- Creating the melody.
  - Begin with either the opening "A" or "B" section.
  - As a class, determine what the feelingful intention for this section will be and which of the musical expressivities (M.U.S.T.S.) will be most useful in creating that feeling.
  - Invite students to read the text aloud. Encourage them speak expressively and note the rise and fall of their voices.
  - Ask students if anyone has a way to sing one of the lines of the text. If no one volunteers, use the "Minute Maker." For one minute all the students in the room sing ideas very quietly, trying as many ideas as they can, repeating the ones they like. The teacher does this, too, but very softly and while looking very thoughtful! At the end of one minute, ask for volunteers or ask if anyone heard any ideas that the group should consider. Invite the composer to sing the idea and the class to echo it.
  - Continue, using the same process that was used for text generation above. When the melody for verse 1 is finished, record it before moving on to another section.

- Repeat this process for the remaining two sections of the song.
- Teacher task: Transcribe the melody and create a simple harmonic accompaniment that supports the students' musical vision to underpin the song.

Session 3—Complimentary Composition, Performance, and Discussion

- Project the lyrics-only or melody-lyrics score.
- Review and sing through the melody.
- Introduce the teacher-created accompaniment and join it with the melody.
- Discuss whether or not the addition of classroom percussion would enhance the song. If parts are added, draw the instruments or the rhythmic notation for what they play on the lyrics-only or melodic score.
- When the students are satisfied with their composition, invite students to take turns performing lead role as soloist while others perform instrumental parts or fill the role of attentive listening audience. Repeat as time allows. Make several recordings.
- Listen to at least one recorded version of the song. Discuss the compositional tools and techniques used to bring about the musical expressivities and feelingful intentions that the class tried to create. Note those things that are most effective on the *Sketchpage*. Remember to add these techniques to classroom anchor charts (See Section 3).

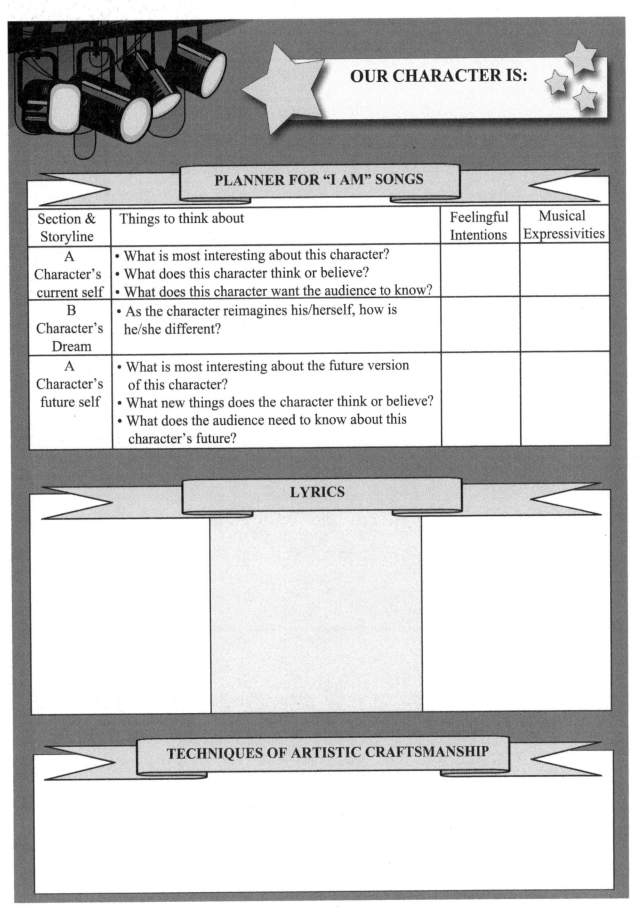

OUR CHARACTER IS:

73

PLANNER FOR "I AM" SONGS

Section & Storyline	Things to think about	Feelingful Intentions	Musical Expressivities
A Character's current self	• What is most interesting about this character? • What does this character think or believe? • What does this character want the audience to know?		
B Character's Dream	• As the character reimagines his/herself, how is he/she different?		
A Character's future self	• What is most interesting about the future version of this character? • What new things does the character think or believe? • What does the audience need to know about this character's future?		

LYRICS

TECHNIQUES OF ARTISTIC CRAFTSMANSHIP

Projects for Grade 4

TONIC AND DOMINANT FRIENDSHIP SONGS

Composition Strand - Songwriting and choral music

About This Project

Friendships are an important part of fourth grade and can be a powerful source of inspiration for young songwriters. In this lesson, students will create Verse-Chorus songs that explore harmony by focusing on the use of tonic and dominant chords. While these chords are easily produced on pitched percussion, most songwriters tend to favor guitar or keyboard. This lesson can also be used with tablet applications that allow students to play chords or pre-program chord patterns.

Materials

- *Sketchpages* with invented, transitional, or traditional notation paper copied onto the "B-side" or made available for students to select as needed
- Guitars, keyboards, or tablets, or other instruments suited to playing tonic and dominant chords

Project Time

- This lesson will take two working sessions. Session 1 will require approximately 20–25 minutes depending on student familiarity with playing chords. Session 2 will take approximately 30 minutes.

Discussion Questions to Develop Compositional Capacities

- Feelingful Intention—How would you describe your friendship?
- Musical Expressivity—What musical sounds would capture the essence of your description? Which of the M.U.S.T.S. would most effectively shape the feelingful impact of the song?

- Artistic Craftsmanship—What are the roles of the V and I chords? What factors influence the decision to use different chords at different points in a song?

Sequence of Activities

Session 1—Introduction and Modeling

- Introduce the "Friendship Song" project. Explain that there are many ways to go about creating a song. Sometimes words come first, sometimes the words and music are created at the same time, and sometimes the melody emerges and then the words.

- Chord Support
  - Begin by talking about the importance of I and V chords in music.
  - Model the two chords.
  - Take a few moments to help the students hear the difference, establishing the I chord as "home" and the V chord as "away, but longing to return."

- Have the students join in playing the chords on guitars, keyboards, or tablet apps. Explore some strumming or chording patterns as shown in Figure 4.1. Once students have gained some performance proficiency, move to lyric writing.

Figure 4.1
Chord patterns
using I and V

I I I I	I I I I	V V V V	I I I I
I I V V	I I V V	I I V V	V V I I
I I I V	I I I V	I I V V	V V I I

- Lyric Writing
  - Invite students to brainstorm on the topic of friendship. How do you feel about your friends? What are things you like to do together? What makes you laugh? Why do you like your friend? Why are friends important? How does it feel to wish you had a friend? List answers where all students can see them.

- Ask the students to discuss the characteristics of good song lyrics. For example, lyrics may
  - have a clear message (usually in the chorus)
  - paint a picture, recreate a feeling, tell a story, or capture a moment
  - use strong verbs and precise nouns
  - employ different types of poetic language such as simile or metaphor
  - use devices such as repetition and alliteration
  - rhyme, but rhyming is not necessary

- Invite the students to play one of the previously practice chord patterns. As they play, use words from the brainstormed list to create a melody and lyric that fits the pattern. After you have modeled a few different possibilities, encourage the students to try to sing their own melodies and lyrics.

- Use one of the sung examples to show students how to notate their ideas as a lead sheet.

Session 2—Partnered Songwriting

- Have the students find partners (individual composers or trios are also acceptable) with whom they can co-write a song about friendship.

- Provide the following task guidelines:
   - Compose a Friendship Song with 1 verse and 1 chorus.
   - Limit the harmonic structure to tonic (I) and dominant (V) chords.
   - Use 20 minutes of composition time.
   - Share songs in class.

- Distribute the *Sketchpage* and encourage students to use it to plan their song. It is helpful to have additional notation sheets available as songs experience a fair number of adjustments and revisions along the way.

- Visit with each composer or team of composers as they work so you can give suggestions about challenges, ask questions, or act as a springboard as students test ideas.

- As soon as students have completed their songs and finished rehearsing them, have them record their songs in a quiet space away from the active music making in the classroom.

- Once all of the songs are recorded, assemble the class to listen to the full "album." Invite composers to share their feelingful intentions. Why did they choose to focus on particular musical expressivities in their song? What was easy or difficult about using tonic and dominant chords?

LEAD SHEET

FRIENDSHIP SONG

Words describing our friendship:

M.U.S.T.S. capturing how our friendship would be expressed:

Tools and techniques for crafting our song:

BEFORE AND AFTER

Composition Strand - Composition and visual media

About This Project

In this activity students will compose music that explores the difference between "before" and "after." Composers are specifically challenged to explore the expressive potentials of "unity and variety." Students will work in small groups to craft music that offers "unity" through features common to both before and after sections of their music while also exhibiting "variety" to highlight how the feelingful quality of two related images or events may differ.

Materials

- The *Sketchpages* for this lesson appear with three different photo pairs so that all students may use the same visual prompt or so that prompts may vary between groups. (Alternatively, students can be invited to bring in pictures that follow the model of the *Sketchpages* provided here.) Invented, transitional, or traditional notation paper should be included on the "B-side" of each sheet or made available for students to use as needed
- Pitched and non-pitched classroom instruments. Students may also use other instruments or electronic sounds as available.

Project Time

- This lesson will occupy one 45-minute class period.

Discussion Questions to Develop Compositional Capacities

- Feelingful Intention—What is the feeling you associate with the before picture? The after picture? How does the feeling change between the two pictures? Why?

- Musical Expressivity—What sounds can be used to capture the change of feeling between the before and after images? For example, might one image suggest a light and high sound while the other suggests a heavier and lower sound?
- Artistic Craftsmanship—What compositional techniques are used to create the sounds that accompany each picture? For example, are the same techniques used with different sounds/instruments? Are sounds/instruments repeated but different techniques applied?

Sequence of Activities

Exploring How Things Change

- Look around the class and select several students who are wearing a similar item of clothing such as a T-shirt. Ask the students to stand. Invite the class to consider what "unifies" these students (makes them similar) and what creates "variety" within the group. See if the class can arrange the students in order—by shirt color, size, graphics, or some other feature.

- Introduce the composition project by drawing a parallel between the unity and variety observed in the students' shirts and the idea that music compositions can share similar characteristics but have differences as well.

- With the students, create an anchor chart or review an existing chart such as that shown in Figure 4.2. Draw attention to the techniques that students have heard composers use to craft unity and variety.

If students need additional exposure to crafting techniques for unity and variety, critical listening activities with theme and variation works may help. Two clear examples for upper elementary students are *American Salute* by Morton Gould and *Variations on Pop Goes the Weasel* by Lucien Cailliet.

- Divide the class into small groups of three to four students and distribute *Sketchpages*.

- Encourage teams to consider the relationship between the "before" and "after" images. Do the two pictures evoke the same feeling or different feelings? These should be noted on the *Sketchpage*. Students should also discuss and make notes addressing these questions:
  - What stays the same in each picture and which sounds might be used to represent unity?
  - What changes between the pictures and sounds might be used to add variety?

Figure 4.2

What we know about how composers craft unity and variety

UNITY	VARIETY
Repeating pitches	Changing pitches
Using the same instrument	Adding or taking away instruments
Using the same melodic shape (high to low pitch)	Changing the melodic shape (high to low pitch followed by low to high pitch)
(continue to develop with students)	*(continue to develop with students)*

- Invite students to collect instruments and begin composing. You will see students testing the sounds their instruments can make, experimenting with musical ideas, repeating ideas, testing ideas, deciding who plays which idea at what point. As teammates agree and disagree in the process, they will learn how musicians work together to form a shared conception of a musical work.

- When the pieces are completed, each team of composers should show their images to the class and perform their pieces. Listeners should be prepared to discuss the compositional techniques used by different groups. Add newly observed craftsmanship techniques to the class unity and variety anchor chart.

84

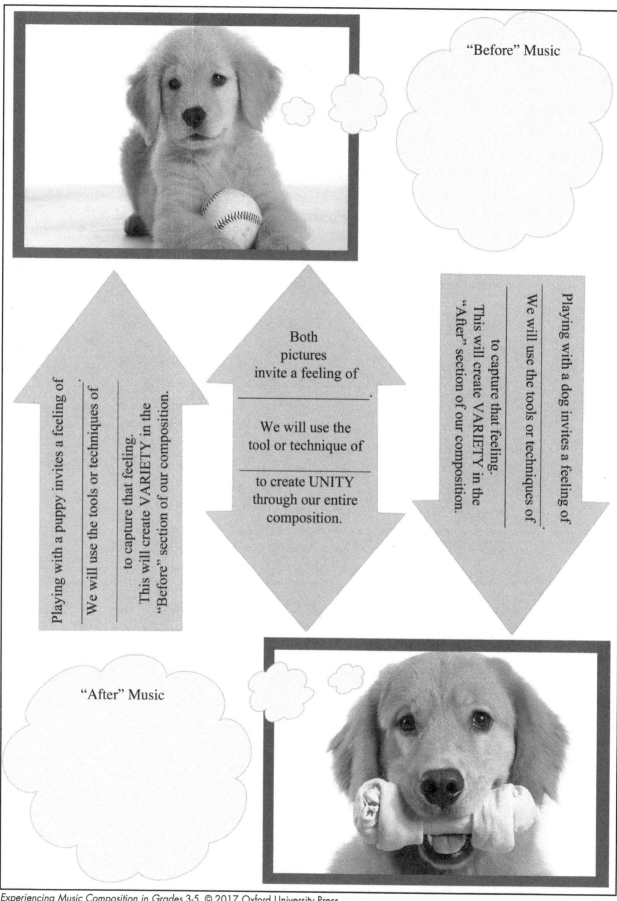

"Before" Music

Playing with a puppy invites a feeling of
_____.
We will use the tools or techniques of
_____
to capture that feeling.
This will create VARIETY in the
"Before" section of our composition.

Both
pictures
invite a feeling of
_____.

We will use the
tool or technique of
_____
to create UNITY
through our entire
composition.

Playing with a dog invites a feeling of
_____.
We will use the tools or techniques of
_____
to capture that feeling.
This will create VARIETY in the
"After" section of our composition.

"After" Music

85

Both pictures invite a feeling of
_____.

We will use the tool or technique of
_____

to create UNITY through our entire
composition.

Waiting for a batch of cookies invites a feeling of
_____.

We will use the tools or techniques of
_____

to capture that feeling.

This will create VARIETY in the
"Before" section of our composition.

Eating cookies with milk invites a feeling of
_____.

We will use the tools or techniques of
_____

to capture that feeling.

This will create VARIETY in the
"After" section of our composition.

Sound ideas...

86

Standing on the
diving board feels
_____.

We will use the tools or techniques of
_____
to capture that feeling.
This will create VARIETY in the
"Before" section of our composition.

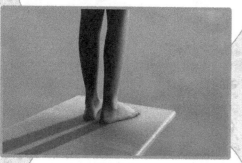

Both pictures invite a feeling of
_____.

We will use the tool or technique of
_____
to create UNITY through our
entire composition.

Sliding into the water after a dive feels
_____.

We will use the tools or techniques of
_____
to capture that feeling.
This will create VARIETY in the
"After" section of
our composition.

Our Before & After music ideas:

PERCUSSION CANON

Composition Strand - Instrumental music

About This Project

Students will work in pairs to create a brief canon for two percussion instruments. Students will create an original rhythm. They then will explore a variety of compositional techniques to determine the feelingful potentials of their rhythm before composing a percussion piece based on their work. Pieces will be performed, analyzed, and discussed.

Materials

- *Sketchpages* and invented, transitional, or traditional notation paper made available for students to select as needed
- Scissors for cutting composition chips from the *Sketchpage*
- A variety of non-pitched percussion instruments with contrasting tone colors, or "found sounds" instruments

Project Time

- It will take approximately 30 minutes to complete this project.

Discussion Questions to Develop Compositional Capacities

- Feelingful Intention—How does the feeling of the music change when different compositional techniques such as unison, call and response, echoing, or canon are used?
- Musical Expressivity—Can all of the M.U.S.T.S. be created when sound sources are limited to just two unpitched percussion instruments?
- Artistic Craftsmanship—How did you structure your piece?

Sequence of Activities

- Begin this composition activity by singing, playing, or listening to a favorite round—a simple canonic form. Discuss how the feeling of the music changes as the unison introduction gives way to the round. What affect is created by the overlapping of lines? Discuss the feeling at the end of the round as each part concludes.

- Have the students form pairs and then invite each pair to select two instruments of contrasting sounds. For example, a pair of students might select a cymbal and a pair of rhythm sticks or a drum and a maraca.

- Invite the students to create a rhythm pattern at least 8 beats long that both can play. Students do not have to notate the rhythm, but they must be able to remember it.

- Begin work with the *Sketchpage* for this activity. Have the students cut the score builder chips from the page. Invite the students to use the chips to experiment with different ways of performing their 8-beat rhythm as a round. Encourage the students arrange the chips in a few different ways. Students should notice how each change affects the feeling of their piece.

- Once students have settled on a chip arrangement that they like, they should practice their canon until they can perform it smoothly.

- When students perform their canon for the class, ask how they arrived at their final arrangement. What feeling did they achieve? Which of the musical expressivities (M.U.S.T.S.) seemed important? What techniques did they find most effective in matching their intentions and instrument choices?

Percussion Canon

Instrument 1	Composing Team Members	Instrument 2

* Work with a partner to compose a percussion canon that is 30-45 seconds in length.
* Begin by selecting two instruments that differ in sound (for example, wood and metal).
* Create a rhythm that is 8 beats long. You may notate it or just remember it, but you must be able to play it together as a canon.
* Cut out the compositional technique chips shown at the bottom of the page.
* Try each compositional technique with your 8-beat rhythm. Determine which techniques best suit your rhythm. You may add technique chips as needed.
* Create a score that shows how your piece will be played. You may use techniques once, more than once, or not at all.
* Be prepared to perform your piece for the class. Discussion questions will include:
  1. What is/are the feelingful intention/s for your composition?
  2. Which of the musical expressivities are most important in shaping the feeling or feelings behind your work?
  3. Of all of the compositional techniques that are used, which one best suits your rhythm? Why?

- - - - - **Cut here** -

Unison	Slower	Forte	Staccato	Start #1 here	Start #2 here
Round	Solo instrument	Piano	Legato	Silence/ Pause	Faster
Call and Response	Echo				

Experiencing Music Composition in Grades 3-5, © 2017 Oxford University Press

HEAD IN THE GAME

Composition Strand - Electronic music and digital media

About This Project

In this lesson, students will consider the impact that music can have on a very particular audience—the gamer engaged in play. As this is a role that many students have filled, they are likely to have a strong intuitive sense of what game music sounds like and what it is meant to accomplish. The students will create a theme for a main character and loops representing three particular actions in a game they imagine. This activity may be completed by students working individually, in pairs, or in groups of three.

Materials

- *Sketchpages* with invented, transitional, or traditional notation paper made available for students to select as needed
- Computers with access to looping software
- Sound equipment for sharing final products

Project Time

- It will take approximately 45 minutes to complete this project.

Discussion Questions to Develop Compositional Capacities

- Feelingful Intention—What feeling will the gamer experience at different points in the game?
- Musical Expressivity—Which of the M.U.S.T.S. is most important in each situation? For example, which might be important if there is a chase scene, or if there is a pause in action as the character decides which of three hallways to enter?
- Artistic Craftsmanship—What style of music is best suited for the game? What sound sources are most likely capture the personality of the main character? Which sound sources will be most effective in sonifying the gamescape?

Sequence of Activities

Begin the lesson by analyzing the music of a few popular video games. Work with the students to determine whether the characters have themes, if different tasks within the game trigger special music, and what each theme or musical idea is supposed to contribute to the experience of the gamer.

Main Character Work

- Give students 1 minute to think about the type of game they would like to invent. Encourage them to consider these questions: Who would be the main character? What is the character trying to achieve? Where would the game take place?

- Have the students complete the first section of the *Sketchpage* where they will
  - draw a quick picture of the main character
  - name the character
  - create a game app icon
  - describe the character's main goal

- Create a theme that captures the main character's personality or some aspect of the challenges in the game. The feelingful intentions, musical expressivities, and techniques of artistic craftsmanship related to the theme should be noted on the *Sketchpage*.

Action Music

- Identify three different actions that would take place in the game. List the three actions and where they take place in the second section of the *Sketchpage*. What would the music for each one sound like? What would make the music sound similar yet allow each action to be distinct?

- Create the loops for each game action. Loops should be about 16 beats in length but may be longer or shorter as suits game action.

Peer Feedback

- Once students have created the theme and loops for their game, they should swap projects with another composer or composing team. The teams should review the game description and listen to the themes and loops. The reviewer should then create a list of "3 stars and 1 wish." The "3 stars" are a list of three things that the composer has done well. A "wish" is something for the composer to think about and consider revising or improving in some way.

- Students should then be given time to revise, if they choose to do so, before projects are shared with the class.

HEAD IN THE GAME

1 DRAW YOUR CHARACTER HERE:

2 NAME YOUR CHARACTER:

3 MAKE A GAME APP ICON

4 THE CHARACTER'S MAIN GOAL IS TO...

5 CREATE A THEME FOR THIS CHARACTER.

WHAT WILL BE THE **FEELINGFUL INTENTION?**

WHICH OF THE **MUSICAL EXPRESSIVITIES** WILL BE MOST IMPORTANT **(M.U.S.T.S.)** ?

WHAT **ARTISTIC CRAFTSMANSHIP** TECHNIQUES WILL YOU USE?

ACTION MUSIC

6 DESCRIBE THREE TASKS OR ACTIONS THAT WILL OCCUR IN THE GAME. **THINK** ABOUT THE FOLLOWING: WHAT IS THE **FEELINGFUL INTENTION** OF THE ACTION? WHICH OF THE **M.U.S.T.S.** WILL BE USED? WHAT **ARTISTIC CRAFTSMANSHIP** TECHNIQUES WILL CREATE THE BEST EXPERIENCE FOR THE GAMER?

94

ACTION 1 IS...
THE F.I. IS...
M.U.S.T.S. ARE...
BEST A.C. IS...

HOW IS THE ACTION MUSIC ALIKE?

ACTION 2 IS...
THE F.I. IS...
M.U.S.T.S. ARE...
BEST A.C. IS...

HOW IS THE ACTION MUSIC DIFFERENT?

ACTION 3 IS...
THE F.I. IS...
M.U.S.T.S. ARE...
BEST A.C. IS...

THERE'S MORE THAN ONE WAY TO TELL A STORY

Composition Strand - Music theater

About This Project

A change in perspective can change everything. In this lesson, students will reimagine a familiar story from the perspective of a prop or minor character. They will use the observations and insights of this prop or minor character to create an "I see" song. This song type is an important theatrical tool as it allows an audience to re-evaluate the main character. Examples of stories modeling perspective change include *The Emperor's New Clothes: An All-Star Retelling of the Classic Fairy Tale* (Starbright Foundation, Houghton Mifflin Harcourt, 1998) where props, articles of clothing, and minor characters share their views, and *The True Story of the Three Little Pigs* by Jon Sciezka and Lane Smith (Puffin Books, 1996) where the story is told from the perspective of the wolf. Given the creative writing aspects of this composition project, it may be used to frame an interdisciplinary collaboration between music and language arts.

Materials

- *Sketchpages* with invented, transitional, or traditional notation paper copied onto the "B-side" or made available for students to select as needed
- A selection of familiar childhood stories and fairy tales
- Classroom instruments (optional: guitars, keyboards, digital sound sources)
- Recording devices

Project Time

- It will take two 30-minute working sessions to complete this project.

Discussion Questions to Develop Compositional Capacities

- Feelingful Intention—How might the feelings of a prop or minor character differ from the feelings and point of view of the main character in the story?
- Musical Expressivity—Which of the M.U.S.T.S. might be most influential in helping the audience empathize with the prop's or minor character's viewpoint?
- Artistic Craftsmanship—How will you use selected compositional technique(s) to strengthen the "I see" message of the prop's or minor character's song?

Sequence of Activities

Session 1

- Discuss the importance of point of view in storytelling. Read or listen to excerpts from *The Emperor's New Clothes, The True Story of the Three Little Pigs,* or any other adaptation that reframes a traditional tale. If using *The Emperor's New Clothes,* it may be helpful to review the writing technique of "personification."

- Help the class select a story that could be expanded. Create a list of minor characters or newly added characters whose perspectives might significantly alter how the audience experiences the story.

- Introduce the composition project and explain that students will be composing "I see"–songs that explore alternative viewpoints.

- Divide the class into partners or groups of three and then have each composing team select a character.

- Distribute *Sketchpages* and have students complete the "New Perspective" portion of the sheet. This provides a foundation for the song they are to compose.

- Once students have considered what their prop or character has to offer, encourage them to return to the "what the audience is going to hear about" section of the *Sketchpage*. The ideas in this section are the starting point for their song lyrics.

Session 2

- Begin class by modeling techniques for songwriting.
  (1) Make up a single line of text and sing it several ways. Use one note per syllable, two or more notes per syllable, or mix the two approaches.
  (2) Play with nonsense syllables by humming and do-doo-doot-ing a melody.
  (3) Say the words as you play melodically on the keyboard (or other instrument) or as you play simple chords. Other ways are possible.

The more examples you provide, the more options the students will consider when they begin to work.

- Show the students how they can draft their song by drawing arrows representing melodic contour over the lyrics.

- Encourage students to sing-compose their song. Some teams may want to write all the lyrics before making up a melody, others will make up music and then add words, and still others will hear lyrics and melody as one unit. All approaches are acceptable.

- Have the students return to their *Sketchpages* to write out lyrics and any other notations that they may need to preserve their work. Encourage students to establish a clear form for their piece. AB forms work well for "before and after" interpretations while "beginning-middle-end" and other forms allow for further elaboration.

- As students complete their work, send them to quiet area of the classroom where they can a make a recording of their song.

- Sharing and Discussion: Take time for each team to share their work with the whole class. Live performance is good, but sometimes students are able to gain more objective distance when they listen to recordings.

- Discuss how each new perspective contributes to the overall story. Analyze the compositional tools and techniques used by each team in sonifying feelingful intention. In what ways did the songwriters' musical choices impact how the audience reacted to the new perspective? Imagine these songs in performance. If all of the songs were to be strung together, what would be the best order? Why?

Optional Extension

- The songs that have been created are centered on a single story and collectively present the opportunity for themed public performance. If concert performance is an option, discuss with the students how they would like to share their work. Would each composition team like to perform its own piece? Would students prefer to have the whole class learn and perform each song? Perhaps a mix of the two approaches? At this point, the teacher and the students should place the pieces in concert order and devise a rehearsal schedule to prepare the works for performance. Students may also be involved in creating posters or other performance promotion activities as composers often engage in these tasks to promote their own music.

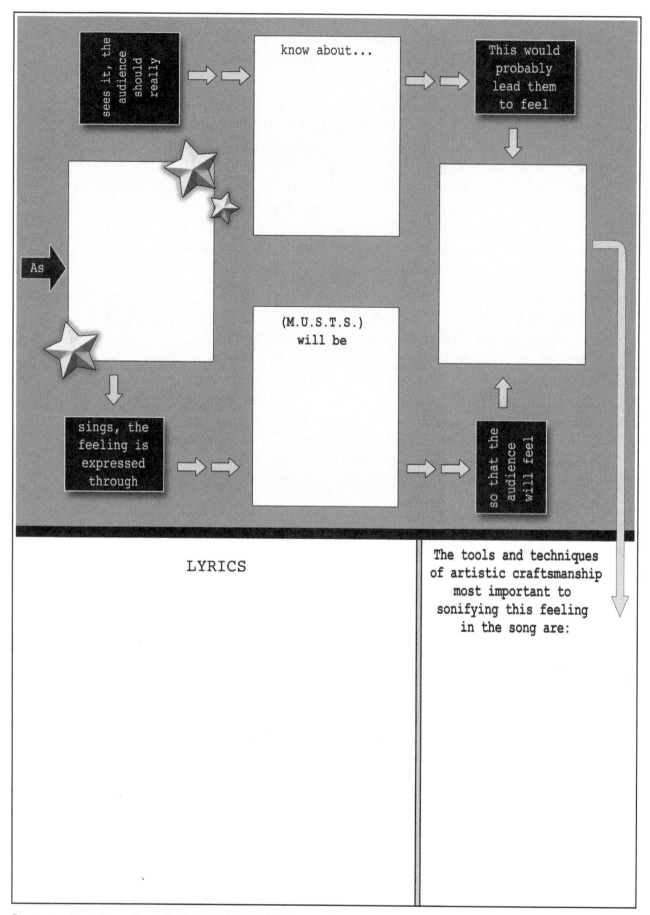

As

sees it, the audience should really

know about...

This would probably lead them to feel

(M.U.S.T.S.) will be

sings, the feeling is expressed through

so that the audience will feel

LYRICS

The tools and techniques of artistic craftsmanship most important to sonifying this feeling in the song are:

Projects for Grade 5

OUR BLUES ALBUM

Composition Strand - Songwriting and choral music

About This Project

The Blues are a common song form ideally suited for introducing students to harmonic writing that includes I, IV, and V chords. In this activity, songwriters will compose a 12-bar Blues, notating melody with chord symbols on a lead sheet. The class will be divided into several small composing teams and the resulting songs will be recorded and compiled into a class-written, produced, and published Blues album.

Materials

- Recordings of at least two 12-bar Blues. The "Good Morning Blues" and "Blues Before Sunrise" are clear examples. For an example where the M.U.S.T.S. are used in complex ways, listen to Ella Fitzgerald's "St. Louis Blues" on Ella Fitzgerald's *Jazz Collection Vol. 8.*
- *Sketchpage,* with traditional notation copied on the "B-side".
- Guitars, or other instruments or tablets with apps for playing chords; Blues backing tracks in multiple keys and tempos can also be found on YouTube.

Project Time

- This project will take approximately three classes to complete: one class to introduce The Blues; one class to compose, notate, and rehearse; and one class to polish and record. This project may be divided into smaller working blocks across five or six class meetings.

Discussion Questions to Develop Compositional Capacities

- Feelingful Intention—What are feelingful intentions commonly associated with The Blues?

- Musical Expressivity—If you were to prioritize the M.U.S.T.S. in order of importance for how you experience The Blues, which would be most important? Least important? Why?
- Artistic Craftsmanship—Blues melodies have pitches that are purposefully lowered to add dramatic weight. How did you decide where to use these pitches in your melody?

Sequence of Activities

Session 1

- Give a brief introduction or review of the Blues:
    - The Blues is a musical form originating from the southern United States.
    - Traits from both traditional African music and European folk music contribute to The Blues.
    - The Blues mixes elements of spirituals, work songs, and narrative ballads to describe troubling times or situations.
    - The Blues come in 8-bar and 16-bar forms, but the 12-bar form is most common.
    - Call-and-response patterns, specific chord progressions, and special scales are key characteristics of the 12-bar Blues.
    - Lyrics from the earliest Blues featured a single line repeated four times.
    - In the early 20th century, the standard pattern became an AAB textual pattern made of one short line sung twice and a longer line sung over the final four measures.
- Have students listen to one or two verses of the "Good Morning Blues." Before playing the example, ask the students to think about how the melody and lyrics work and how many chords are used. Ask them to identify any other compositional techniques they hear. Gather student responses.
- Discuss the content of lyrics. What are the lyrics about? What kind of story do they tell? What did the composer or performer do to make the lyrics interesting?
- Following observations of the chordal construction, introduce the I, IV, and V chords by playing them on a guitar or piano. Play a few different patterns and have students identify the chords by numerical name.
- Listen to one verse of the "Blues Before Sunrise" and have students hold up one, four, or five fingers as they hear the chords change. Note the student responses in graphic form.
- Project the 12-bar Blues graph shown in Figure 4.3 so that the whole class can see it. Ask students to point and "air trace" the graph as another verse is played. Note the harmonic tension between I and higher chords. Encourage students to feel the tension or "weight" of IV and V and the release of I.
- For classes with guitars or keyboards, teach students to play the progression.

Chords												
					IV	IV			V	IV		
	I	I	I	I			I	I			I	I*
Measure	1	2	3	4	5	6	7	8	9	10	11	12

*The I-chord at the end of the Blues progression may be replaced with a V-chord to lead to the next verse.

Figure 4.3
Chord progression for 12-bar Blues

103

Session 2

- Project the lyrics of the "Good Morning Blues." Invite the students to make observations about construction and content. They will likely notice that the lyrics are organized in an AAB form that features a repeated question and a response.

> *Good morning, Blues. Blues, how do you do?*
> *Good morning Blues. Blues, how do you do?*
> *I'm doing all right. Good morning. How are you?*

- Practice lyric writing. Model using a topic familiar to the students. Ask students for evocative adjectives and phrases that describe how they feel about the topic. Have the students turn these ideas into singable phrases.

- Once the lyrics are set, play a Blues progression in the background and invite the students to simultaneously and quietly test melodic ideas. Either ask for volunteers to sing their melodies or walk around the room and listen for interesting tunes that you can sing to the class. Guide students in selecting the most compelling melodies. When the three phrases are complete, sing them a few times and then record.

- Show the class how the song would look on a lead sheet: lyrics, melody notated, chords written above.

- Discuss what a "concept album" is and have the class determine a focus concept for an album—for example, songs about homework, or vegetables, or an upcoming significant event.

- Allow students to work individually, with partners, or in groups of three, to create their own Blues. If performing chords on guitar or piano is too challenging, provide students access to backing tracks. Students should create lead sheets for their compositions.

Session 3

- Rehearse pieces and record final products. Bind a book of lead sheets for the class as a memento.

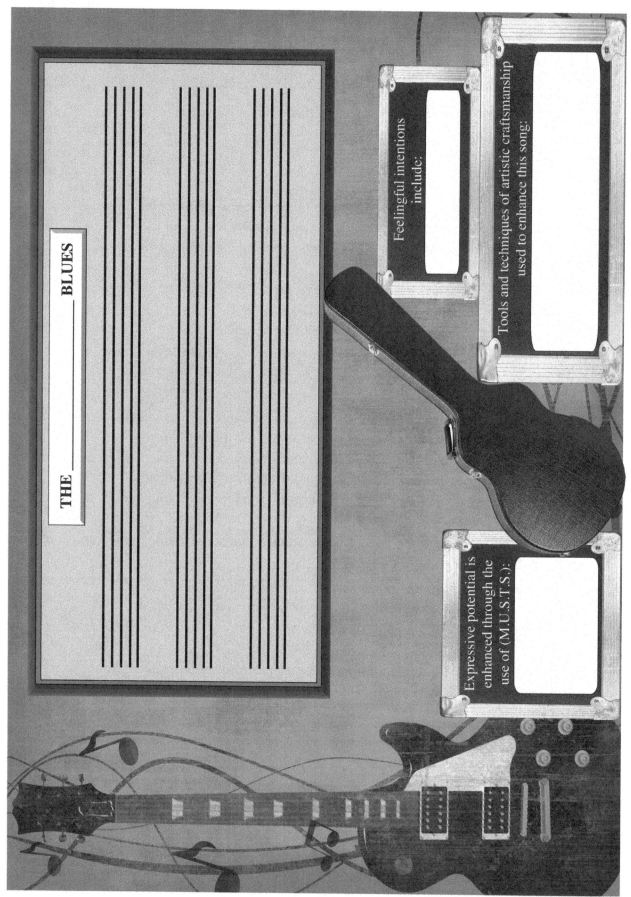

FROM SILENT MOVIE TO FILM SCORE
Just "Say Cheese"

Composition Strand - Composition and visual media

About This Project

Film scoring invites students to move beyond creating sound effects and character themes to create music that enhances all aspects of a story. Film music is usually unobtrusive and, if done well, the audience often experiences it without always noticing its presence. In this activity the composers will create music to accompany a short film.

Note: A variety of public domain films may be found at http://www.archive.org. Video shorts can be related to other curricular areas. Time-lapse videography enhances science and science fair presentations. Videos created in the style commonly associated with Ken Burns can augment history and history fair exhibits. See http://www.pbs.org/kenburns for examples.

Materials

- *Sketchpages* with invented, transitional, or traditional notation paper copied onto the "B-side" or made available for students to select as needed
- Brief movie or cartoon clip with interesting music
- A movie of 1–2 minutes in length with a strong storyline. "Say Cheese," directed and animated by Derek Flood, is available in several file formats through http://www.archive.org.

Time

- It will take approximately 45 minutes to complete this project.

Discussion Questions to Develop Compositional Capacities

- Feelingful Intention—What feelings should be heightened for the audience in each scene?
- Musical Expressivity—Which of the M.U.S.T.S. seem important in each scene? In the transitions between scenes?
- Artistic Craftsmanship—What sounds will have the biggest impact in supporting the characters, actions, or overall story? How will these sounds affect each scene? What sounds will be used to provide unity across the film as well the variety needed to make each scene unique?

Sequence of Activities

Movie Analysis

- View a brief movie or cartoon clip with interesting music (Note: Do not use "Say Cheese" for this step.) Play the clip without music and then with music. Discuss why the students prefer to view the clip with or without music. Note how music is used to enhance the storyline. When and where does the music change and why?
- With the sound turned off, watch and analyze "Say Cheese." Have students identify the big scenes and transitions as they consider the following:
  - What is the overall message of the story?
  - What brings about change?
  - How can music be used to enhance the overall message and to signify changes?
  - Note: Although film scoring and the creation of sound effects involve two different types of artists (composers and Foley artists), ask the students to identify any sounds that might be expected by the audience. These might include hopping, drooling, burping, or kitten mewing, etc. These sounds occur in specific spots and may influence musical choices.

Collaborative Scoring

- Divide the class into small groups and distribute *Sketchpages*. Once initial ideas are drafted, students should collect instruments or tablets and begin to compose. While professional composers create dozens of tiny musical ideas and gestures to accompany actions that may be just 1–2 seconds in length within a larger section, students will think more globally. They will be able to compose the music for 30 seconds of film in just 8–10 minutes.
- Film and recorded score can be merged in electronic formats.
- View movies and discuss how different musical interpretations alter how the audience engages with the story and characters. Consider making a "best ideas" score by extracting highlights from every small group's score to compile a "master score." Does this master score work? Why or why not?

Optional Extension

- Have students create short films of their own and compose the score for them.

- Movie night! Repeat the project with each team working on its own movie short. When the compositions are complete, host a movie night for friends and family. Recorded performance and films can be merged, but this might also be an opportunity for students to perform live, as musicians did in the days of silent films. Remember the popcorn!

SAY CHEESE

Movie frame start time:

Feelingful intention:

Musical expressivity:

Artistic craftsmanship:

Movie frame start time:

Feelingful intention:

Musical expressivity:

Artistic craftsmanship:

Movie frame start time:

Feelingful intention:

Musical expressivity:

Artistic craftsmanship:

SOUNDSCAPES
A Walk through the Fair

Composition Strand - Instrumental music

About This Project

The observations that students make as they walk through street fairs or country fairs can provide an interesting source of inspiration for young composers. The goal of the activity is to sonify the experience of attending a fair. This activity, designed for composers with some previous experience in composition and small-group work, will allow a whole class to create a musical score for a walk through a street or county fair. Students will be challenged to think about what it feels like to smell the smells, see the sights, experience the exhilarating speed and height of carnival rides, or watch jugglers or clowns on stilts. They will explore how these feelings can be captured in sound so that others might better understand the experience of visiting a fair.

Materials

- *Sketchpages*; separate sheets of invented, transitional, or traditional notation paper made available for students to use as needed
- Classroom instruments or beginning ensemble instruments
- Scissors to cut fairground "snapshots" and path guides from the *Sketchpage*
- Large display board and magnets, tacks, or tape for hanging "snapshots" and path guides
- Optional: audio recording device

Project Time

- It will take approximately 45 minutes to complete this project.

Questions to Develop Compositional Capacities

- Feelingful Intention—How does it feel to walk through a fair and experience the various aspects of it? Is there an overarching feeling of a fair? Do individual attractions leave different feelingful impressions?
- Musical Expressivity—Which of the M.U.S.T.S. best captures the feeling of each attraction at the fair? Are there attractions that draw on multiple M.U.S.T.S.?
- Artistic Craftsmanship—Which sounds will best portray specific fairground attractions and events? Are there particular techniques that can be used to create a sense of the fair as a whole as well as the individual attractions?

Sequence of Activities

Introduction

- Discuss what it is like to go to the fair. If students have not attended a fair, read a book about going to the fair and show pictures or videos of different types of fairs. Discuss what it would be like to visit a fair.

- Construct a map of an agricultural fair or a street fair. Where would visitors enter? What attractions would they encounter? Encourage students to consider what they might find for display tents or buildings, food options, livestock, gaming, and rides.

- Explain the composition project to the students. The class will collaborate to create a theme and then each team will create a short piece, just 20–30 seconds in length, representing one attraction. The score will be constructed by placing pictures of the attractions on a map. The music will be "played" in the order determined by a conductor—a visitor to the fair who follows the map. Different visitors will walk through the fair in different ways so that different arrangements of the music will be made from the same set of attractions.

The "Walking Theme"

- Introduce the concept of a "walking theme." This theme can be used to provide unity to the class composition. Help the class create the theme by asking the following questions:
  - What is the feeling you get when you walk through a fairground?
  - How can you make that feeling with sounds?
  - Will the musical idea that you have created help someone else feel like he or she is walking through the fair?
  - Note: If students need to hear a model of walking music, Virgil Thompson's "Walking Song" from the *Louisiana Story: Acadian Songs and Dances* can be used to demonstrate how music can be created to suggest an interesting walk.

- If students find this task to be challenging, encourage them to begin with a rhythmic idea and then move to the creation of a melody. Other questions a teacher might ask include these:
    - Will the theme have continuous motion or will there be pauses?
    - Will the theme be stable (predictable)?
    - Will it be smooth or jaunty?
    - Will we sing it or play it on instruments—or both?
- As ideas emerge for the walking theme, have the full class echo-perform each idea. Discuss the musical potentials of each idea and select one to be the "walking theme."

Composing for Fair Attractions

- Divide students into teams of two to three members and have them select an attraction to sonify. Each group should have a different attraction.
- Have teams work with the *Sketchpage* to make a quick drawing of their chosen attraction and then to consider the feelingful intentions, musical expressivities, and artistic craftsmanship components of their composition. Encourage students to avoid merely creating sound effects. Each attraction should have a distinct piece of music representative of how the team feels, or how they imagine someone might feel, when visiting that attraction.
- Give the students a few minutes to work and then circulate to each group. If teams are struggling, prompt students to think about their compositions by asking questions that invite critical analysis and reflection:
    - What is the feeling that you are trying to evoke?
    - What sounds are you using to evoke that feeling?
    - What do you think the audience will feel when they hear your music?

Putting It All Together

- When all of the composing teams have completed their compositions, draw students back to full-class work. Using a large display board, have students lay out walking paths and attractions using their drawn attraction and footprints cut from their *Sketchpage*.
- Review the walking theme and then attempt a performance of *A Walk through the Fair* with the teacher filling the role of conductor. If possible, record the performance of the piece. This is an important step if this lesson extends to another class period.
- Using the map as a guide, ask each group to identify their compositional intention and how they tried to achieve it. Invite the students to indicate how successful they were at crafting their musical ideas. Highlight strong compositional work by inviting the class to comment on effective musical ideas.
- To close the activity, encourage students to evaluate their work by imagining possible improvements and revisions. The teacher might ask questions similar to these:
    - If we were to do this again, how might we improve this piece?

o Is there sufficient unity and variety in the music as we walk through the fair? If so, how did we achieve it? If not, how could we revise our piece so that it more effectively uses unity and variety to hold the listener's attention?

Optional Extension 1—Student Conductors and Arrangements

• Return to the project with "Today we are going to revisit our musical fairground and some of you will be able to conduct our *A Walk through the Fair* piece. Let's listen to the recording of our last performance to consider what worked well and what we might improve." Discuss.

• Give students 5 minutes to work in their groups to make any desired changes.

• Refocus the class and discuss what a conductor will need to think about while leading the performance. Questions may include these:
   o How fast will you walk? Will you pause? Will your pace slow as you get tired?
   o How might you show that you are waiting in line?
   o Will you walk through each section of the fair just once or will you repeat sections that you liked?

• Select a volunteer student-conductor and fill in as a performer within the small group. Perform the piece, repeating the analysis and discussion with each new arrangement.

• Discuss which path through the fair creates the most effective musical piece.

Optional Extension 2

• Mussorgsky's *Pictures at an Exhibition* may be used to further explore compositions ordered by events. The work, inspired by an exhibition of watercolors by Viktor Hartmann, explores locales in Poland, France, and Italy and concludes with music inspired by the architectural design for the capital city of Ukraine. Though some of the original art works have been lost, several are readily available as prints that can be shared with students. Of particular interest for expanding students' notions of a walking theme is movement eight in which the theme shifts from functioning as a unifying device and becomes a key component of the "Cum mortuis in lingua mortua" movement. Listening questions and activities might include these:
   o Listen to the first movement, "Promenade." How did Mussorgsky create the feel of walking?
   o Show examples of Hartmann's paintings and listen to Mussorgsky's musical portrayals. How did Mussorgsky capture the characteristics of each scene depicted by Hartmann?
   o Share the story of the work's creation. Listen to a few segments without pause. Why is there silence between segments?
   o Listen to any segment of the work in its original form (piano only) and then as orchestrated by Ravel. How does changing instrumentation alter how we experience the work?

Ideas for music...

Draw the attraction.

The tools and techniques of artistic craftsmanship that invite this experience are:

The musical expressivities that will play the most important role are:

The feelingful intentions that best fit this attraction are:

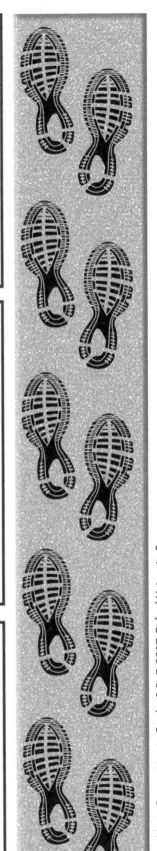

Experiencing Music Composition in Grades 3-5, © 2017 Oxford University Press

PODCASTS WITH PEER COMPOSERS

Composition Strand - Electronic music and digital media

About This Project

Just as adult composers are sometimes interviewed about their works or present pre-concert lectures to educate curious audience members, young composers can be asked to comment on their compositions. As part of this project, students fill the roles of interviewer and interviewee as they learn to describe their works and working processes to others.

In this lesson, students create individual pieces in a digital format using looping software. They are challenged to create pieces that contain at least two contrasting ideas in a logical form. When the compositions are complete, students partner with a peer composer to listen critically to each other's pieces. They then create questions about the work, interview each other, and create a podcast featuring musical excerpts interspersed with interview.

Some students may wish to produce videocasts. This is certainly an option, but video can create a distraction. For the purposes of this lesson, it is important for students to focus on the music and the composer's thoughts about it. If videocasting is used, it will require additional guidelines.

Materials

- *Sketchpages* with invented, transitional, or traditional notation paper made available for students to use, if needed
- Access to digital sound software with looping and recording capabilities

Project Time

- It will take approximately 90 minutes to complete this project.

Discussion Questions to Develop Compositional Capacities

- Feelingful Intention—What feeling are you trying to evoke in this piece? How will your contrasting section feel differently?
- Musical Expressivity—Which of M.U.S.T.S. pairs are most important in creating the contrast within your piece? Which of the M.U.S.T.S. play supporting roles?
- Artistic Craftsmanship—What are the key features of your composition? Are there any special or unique compositional techniques used? What influenced your choice of loops or other sounds as used in your composition?

Sequence of Activities

Composition Phase

- Students will work individually with looping software to create a 60–90 second piece with two contrasting ideas. They need to know how to create tracks, arrange loops, record external sounds, and save their work.
- Composition work may be completed in class or as homework, but it is important to allow composers to work on their pieces until they feel they are finished.
- Include opportunities for peer feedback in Composers' Circles and allow for revision.
- When compositions are complete, pair students and have them exchange compositions for analysis.

Analysis of Peer Compositions and Planning the Interview

- Take time to have a brief class discussion about the analysis of peer works and interview preparation. In many ways, analysis will parallel the feedback parameters used in Composers' Circles.
- Collaboratively create a set of analysis guidelines that might include the following:
  - Write a general description of the piece
  - Identify the key features of the work—formal organizations, instrumentation, etc.
  - Identify the unique use of musical materials
- Discuss audience curiosity. What do people want to know about composers, their work, and their music? Brainstorm a list of possible topics that interviewers can adapt to fit their particular composer and composition. Students should plan a podcast of approximately 4 minutes in length. Interview questions and answers interspersed with musical excerpts will occupy about 2 minutes. The 60–90-second composition should be played in full near the end of the segment.

- At this point, make 2-minute appointments with each student to see what each has found in his or her analysis and what each has created for interview questions. Offer guidance as needed to help students expand, narrow, or refine their work. Alternatively, if individual meetings cannot be scheduled, collect student work, review, and return with written comments.

Conducting Interviews

- Assist students in setting up external microphones and have them make test recordings. If possible, set up one corner of the room as quiet zone for recording. USB headsets with microphones work well and reduce external noise.

- Have students conduct and record interviews. Encourage them to ask more questions than they think they will need. Recorded materials will be edited.

Editing and Publishing Podcasts

- Using the *Sketchpage*, students should create a timeline for their podcasts. They will need to create some additional musical material as well as select and plan the placement of compositional excerpts and interview segments.

- Once completed, these podcasts can be shared with parents and others on a class website.

Optional Extension

- The podcasts could serve as introductions to the pieces for a concert of student works.

- Podcasts could be projected in a performance space as "pre-concert lectures" as the audience settles in and awaits the beginning of a student concert.

118

Podcasts with Peer Composers

Create Original Composition

- [ ] work individually
- [ ] 60-90 seconds in length
- [ ] use looping software
- [ ] may record audio tracks
- [ ] must contain two contrasting ideas

Feelingful intentions?

Musical expressivities?

Artistic craftsmanship?

Listen to and Analyze Peer Composition

- [ ] General observations

- [ ] Key features

- [ ] Unique musical ideas and time range where they happen

- [ ] Other...

Podcasts with Peer Composers

Prepare and Conduct Interview

☐ Questions I will ask:

1.

2.

3.

4.

5.

others:

_____

☐ Test microphone
☐ Sound level check for interviewer and interviewee

Create Podcast

☐ Create and position intro music with fade out transition to "Welcome to today's show."

☐ Select, edit, and position excerpts of the featured composition.

☐ Select, edit, and position excerpts of the interview.

☐ Position the full-length composition, leaving time at the end for a closing. Position closer: "Thank you to our composer, [insert name], for sharing [insert title] with us today."

☐ Create and position outro music with fade-in transition.

| 0:00 | 4:00 |

THE MINI-MUSICAL
A Story in Just Five Songs

Composition Strand - Musical theater

About This Project

Musical theater productions take audiences on an emotional roller coaster, manipulating their feelings and desires as they meet characters and watch a story unfold. This project will draw on what students know about how music enriches movies, television, and live action plays as students create a mini-musical based on a familiar story. The activities of the project will include an overview and the creation of five different types of theater songs: character songs, ballads, charm songs, comedic songs, and closing/big finish songs.

Materials

- *Sketchpages* for character songs, ballads, charm songs, comedic songs, and closing/big finish songs with invented, transitional, or traditional notation paper copied onto the "B-side" or made available for students to select as needed
- A selection of familiar stories and fairy tales
- Classroom instruments (optional: guitars, keyboards, or digital sound sources)

Project Time

- It will take approximately 6–8 working sessions to complete this project.

Discussion Questions to Develop Compositional Capacities

- Feelingful Intention—The five songs serve different functions within the musical. What types of feelingful intentions seem best suited to each song type? To the specific songs of this composition project?

- Musical Expressivity—Which of the M.U.S.T.S. will be most useful in shaping the feelingful impact of each song? How might the use of different M.U.S.T.S. contribute to the overall dramatic impact of the storyline being used in this project?
- Artistic Craftsmanship—What are the functional and relational roles of the songs within the play? What factors influence the choice of tools and techniques at different points in a song and within the musical as whole?

Sequence of Activities

Part One—Concepts and Models

- Discuss what makes a good story and list the characteristics described by the students.

- Introduce the mini-musical project and discuss who the intended audience will be (grade level classmates, full elementary school, parents and siblings, etc.).

- Keeping these criteria in mind, discuss with the class existing stories that could be made into a mini-musical. Note: It is usually best to avoid stories that are already films or musicals as these can influence the composers and make it difficult for them to be original in their work.

- To learn about how songs are used in musicals, invite the class to identify songs they know from musicals or musical films. Listen to several songs and analyze when the song appears in the story and what its purpose is. Have at least one example ready to share from each category described below:
  - Character songs tell what the character is thinking or feeling. They may move the plot forward and hint at or reveal hidden qualities of the character. Character songs can be "I want" or "I am" songs. Examples include "In My Own Little Corner" from Rodgers and Hammerstein's *Cinderella*; "I Feel Pretty" from *West Side Story*; "For Good" from *Wicked*; and "Suppertime" from *You're a Good Man, Charlie Brown*.
  - Ballads are slower, thoughtful pieces that often highlight a relationship between two characters. They are usually presented in verse and chorus form and tell some part of the story or move the action forward. Examples include "Candle on the Water" from *Pete's Dragon*; "Look to the Rainbow" from *Finian's Rainbow*; "Castle on a Cloud" from *Les Misérables*; and "Somewhere, Out There" from *An American Tale*.
  - Comedic songs offer a chance to lighten or change the mood. They serve to set things up for the crisis or resolution of the crisis in the storyline. These songs are usually faster and more rhythmic than other song types. Examples include "Be Our Guest" from *Beauty and the Beast*; "Trouble" from *The Music Man*; "Popular" from *Wicked*; and "Hakuna Matata" from *The Lion King*.
  - Charm songs beguile the audience and lead them to develop a particular opinion about a character. Examples include "Wouldn't It Be Lovely" from *My Fair Lady*; and "Stay Awake" from *Mary Poppins*.

○ The Big Finish/Closer is an uplifting number often sung by the entire cast. This song summarizes the main theme of the play (story) and often starts in one musical mood (more somber and reflective) then changes to an up tempo and highly rhythmic joyous conclusion. Closers often reprise a song from earlier in the show. Examples include "76 Trombones" from *The Music Man*; "Circle of Life" from *The Lion King*; and "Happiness" from *You're a Good Man, Charlie Brown*.

Part Two—Creating a Story and Song Board

- Using the selected story as a guide, discuss where the best places might be to place a character song, ballad, comedic song, charm song, and the big finish/closer. Map out a rough plan for where each song will occur in the story.

- Discuss with the class the purpose of each song. Are there places where the songs should sound similar or be reprised? Which songs need to contrast to highlight the action of the story? Which character or characters will sing each song?

- Divide the class into composing teams. Groups of three to five composers are most efficient. Determine which group will work on which song. The length of the songs will influence how long it takes each group to complete its work. If students concentrate on lyrics and melody, songs may come together quite quickly. If students are working with acoustic or smart device instruments to build accompaniments, more time will be needed.

- Regardless of song length, the creative process includes task defining, idea generation, idea testing, idea selection/rejection, and repetition of this process until a completed product emerges. Encourage students to use strategies that they have used in earlier projects to write lyrics, compose melodies, and craft accompaniments that capture the feelingful intention of their number in the show.

Part Three—Words and Music

- It is preferable for the teacher or a small group of students with strong writing skills to prepare the script as whole class writing can be long and tedious work. This task could be completed outside of class or might be a project component shared with and led by a language arts teacher.

- Once songs are drafted, the script should be read with the songs inserted so that the students may evaluate how the music works within the story. During this process, it is important to focus on the overall flow of the story and song placement rather than the specific musical ideas of the composers.

- Decide where additional music may be needed. Is music needed to set the mood at the beginning? As background to any dialogue? To accompany any of the action?

Part Four—Get a Job!

- Divide the class into working groups for creating the rest of the production. One fun way of deciding who does what is to have everyone apply for his or her favorite three jobs. Design a simple job application and have the students write about why they want a particular job and why they think they will be good at it. Musicians and actors could audition for a panel of judges, comprised of teachers, for such jobs as these:
    - Musicians who create and play the music as suggested above. This usually involves about five people.
    - Actors, as needed. Usually three to four, maybe more.
    - A publicity team of two to three students to make posters, programs, and tickets.
    - Electricians who handle aspects of running lights. This is a good place to enlist the assistance of another teacher.
    - Costumers can create the costumes to be worn. The assistance of a parent-volunteer can be helpful to students fulfilling this role.
    - Stage crew including a property master and assistant to handle props and a prompter to help forgetful actors with lines.
    - Other ideas are possible. Everyone in class should have a valuable job and appear on stage at the end for a curtain call.

Part Five—Putting It All Together

- Rehearse the play. It may take three to four complete run-throughs for all the students to learn to do their jobs effectively. The final day before the first performance needs to be a dress rehearsal with full costumes, lighting, and music unfolding in real time.

Part Six—Performance

- If possible, there should be two or three performances and a video should be made—the perfect job for one or two budding videographers.

Part Seven—Celebration and Reflection

- Pop the corn and watch the video. Discuss what worked well and point out all that students learned in the process. Celebrate the accomplishments!

Optional Extensions

- Students create the story themselves instead of using a familiar one.
- Students compose original music for a musical that already exists. This can be a real challenge, but it leads to an understanding that there is more than one way to set texts.

LYRICS

CHARACTER SONGS help the audience understand what a character wants or who a character is.

The song lyrics may even use the words "I am" or "I want" to tell the character's story.

✓ What should the audience know about this character?

✓ How will the audience feel before and after they know who the character is or what he or she wants?

✓ How will the use of M.U.S.T.S. change across the song to help the audience's impression of the character change?

✓ Ideas for sounds and techniques that can help shape the audience's reaction:

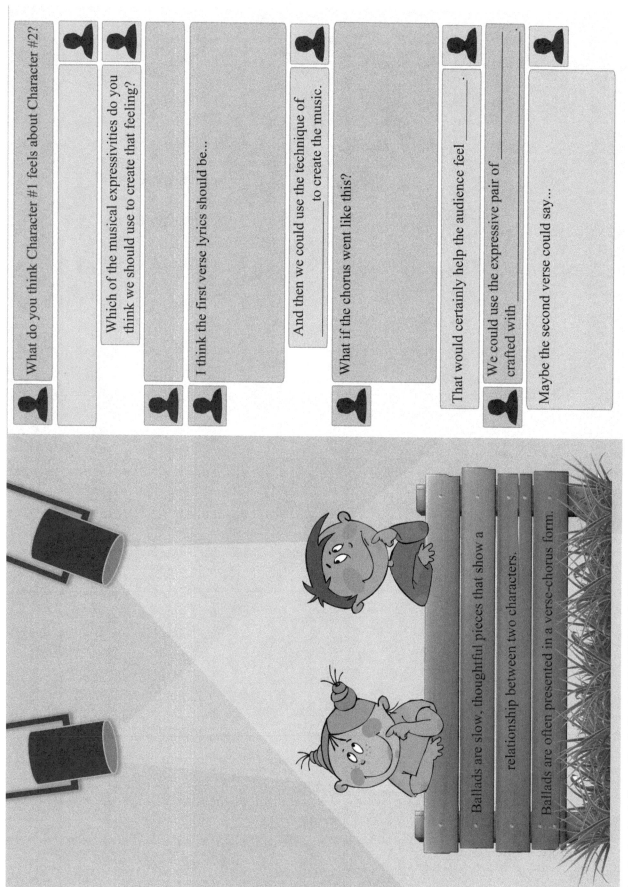

126

What do you think Character #1 feels about Character #2?

Which of the musical expressivities do you think we should use to create that feeling?

I think the first verse lyrics should be...

And then we could use the technique of _____ to create the music.

What if the chorus went like this?

That would certainly help the audience feel _____.

We could use the expressive pair of _____ crafted with _____.

Maybe the second verse could say...

Ballads are slow, thoughtful pieces that show a relationship between two characters.

Ballads are often presented in a verse-chorus form.

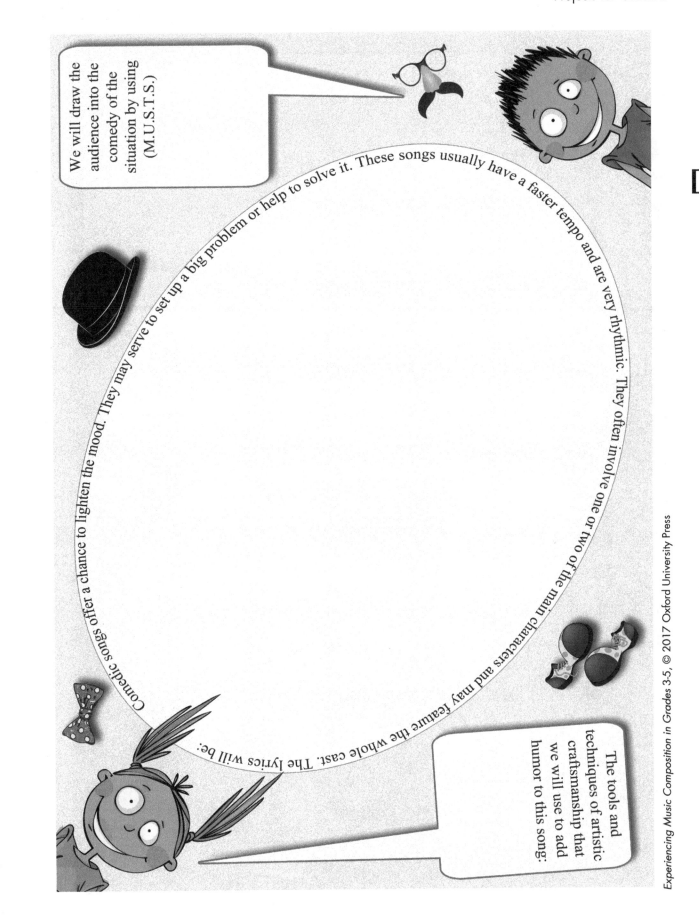

We will draw the audience into the comedy of the situation by using (M.U.S.T.S.)

Comedic songs offer a chance to lighten the mood. They may serve to set up a big problem or help to solve it. These songs usually have a faster tempo and are very rhythmic. They often involve one or two of the main characters and may feature the whole cast. The lyrics will be:

The tools and techniques of artistic craftsmanship that we will use to add humor to this song:

Experiencing Music Composition in Grades 3-5, © 2017 Oxford University Press

INCIDENTAL MUSIC PLANNER

Music that happens in the background of a scene is called "incidental music." It exists to add atmosphere. Incidental music can be as simple as a single tone or as complex as needed to support action or advance the story.

	Scene	Feelingful Intention	Musical Expressivities	Artistic Craftsmanship
	Scene	Feelingful Intention	Musical Expressivities	Artistic Craftsmanship
	Scene	Feelingful Intention	Musical Expressivities	Artistic Craftsmanship
	Scene	Feelingful Intention	Musical Expressivities	Artistic Craftsmanship
	Scene	Feelingful Intention	Musical Expressivities	Artistic Craftsmanship

APPENDIX: *SKETCHPAGE* NOTATION TEMPLATES

Title:

Composer(s):

for composers using invented or iconographic notations

Title:

Composer(s):

for composers using invented or iconographic notations in partnership with traditional notation
(best as memory booster before part alignment is desired)

Experiencing Music Composition in Grades 3-5, © 2017 Oxford University Press

Title:

Composer(s):

for scores using invented or iconographic notations in partnership with traditional notation (best for aligning parts)

Experiencing Music Composition in Grades 3-5, © 2017 Oxford University Press

Title:

Composer(s):

for composers using traditional notation